Public Sphere

Síreacht: Longings for Another Ireland is a series of short, topical and provocative texts on controversial issues in contemporary Ireland.

Contributors to the *Síreacht* series come from diverse backgrounds and perspectives but share a commitment to the exposition of what may often be disparaged as utopian ideas, minority perspectives on society, polity and environment, or critiques of received wisdom. Associated with the phrase *ceól sírechtach síde* found in Irish medieval poetry, *síreacht* refers to yearnings such as those evoked by the music of the *aos sí*, the supernatural people of Irish mythology. As the title for this series, we use it to signify longings for and imaginings of a better world in the spirit of the World Social Forums that 'another world is possible'. At the heart of the mythology of the *sí* is the belief that laying beneath this world is the other world. So too these texts address the urgent challenge to imagine potential new societies and relationships, but also to recognise the seeds of these other worlds in what already exists.

Other published titles in the series are

Freedom? by Two Fuse
Commemoration by Heather Laird

The editors of the series, Órla O'Donovan, Fiona Dukelow and Rosie Meade, School of Applied Social Studies, University College Cork, welcome suggestions or proposals for consideration as future titles in the series. Please see http://sireacht.ie/ for more information.

Public Sphere

HARRY BROWNE

Series Editors:
Órla O'Donovan, Fiona Dukelow and Rosie Meade

CORK **CUP** UNIVERSITY PRESS

First published in 2018 by
Cork University Press
Youngline Industrial Estate
Pouladuff Road, Togher
Cork T12 HT6V, Ireland

British Library Cataloguing in Publication Data
A CIP catalogue record for this book is available from the British
Library.

ISBN 9781782052432

Typeset by Studio 10 Design
Printed by Hussar Books in Poland

CONTENTS

Introduction

L ike many journalists, I've had the sobering experience of writing something that I thought was pretty good, then meeting a 'civilian' who knows much more about the subject on which I've just pontificated. Sometimes it's someone whose expertise is of the professional variety: the cryptographer who casually cuts holes in my published conclusions about the safest apps for secure mobile messaging, say. More often, and worse, it's someone who has no remunerative reason to be more informed than me, but is anyway: the maths teacher who enthusiastically rattles off the playlist of the gig I've just reviewed, when I'd been pleased to recognise three of the songs; the plumber who knows chapter and verse on all of Charlie Haughey's scandals, which I've just summarised with what I now realise, too late, was a less-than-apt generalisation.

The vast majority of the time, these people are nice about it, at least to my face. Often it's clear they haven't read my articles closely enough to notice I was wrong or at least ignorant: their expertise flows freely after a friendly 'I saw you were writing about ...'. This allows me to quietly thank my lucky stars that they do not seem inclined to write stern, corrective letters to the editor, and to hope that there are not too many other experts out there who just might. By and large, people who know a lot about a subject, especially an obscure one, seem okay about the non-expertise of journalists in that area. The funny thing, though, is that they generally appear to assume that it's their area alone that defeats us, and that we revert to perfectly assured accuracy and reliability about everything else. It's a relatively benign variation on the old story about Elton John reading a tabloid newspaper, aghast at the blatantly fabricated lies it is telling about his private life, then turning the page and declaring, 'Oh, I see Madonna has a new lover.'

Even if we're not inclined to fabricate or to believe malicious leaks, the dance along the brink of authority, always fearing a fall into the abyss of ignorance, is hard to avoid for journalists. As I've often told students who are writing a poorly paid freelance article: if they've gathered a lot of information that won't fit in the word-count, that's called 'over-research'. (Many's the newspaper journalist who has to do extra, frantic post-publication research in order to talk coherently about their story on the radio.) From a reporter's point of view, this brinksmanship is part of the upside of the much-derided 'herd mentality' and the reliance on a small, familiar set of elite sources of information: if we're wrong, at least we'll all be wrong together.

I offer this confession on behalf of myself and my quasi-erstwhile profession for two reasons. One is to suggest that even in the best of circumstances, and leaving all questions of power out of the picture, the agglomeration of highly contingent (not to say half-assed and bluffing) knowledge that journalism provides is perhaps a weak foundation on which to rest the edifice of a democracy. The undoubted fact that the media provide us with things to talk about, to get angry about, to laugh about, to mourn about, to argue about, does not mean they constitute a deliberative public sphere – a space or series of spaces where, the theory goes, public issues can be sensibly discussed and consensus on them developed. As we expand our understanding of media, and of a putative public sphere, to incorporate posts and debates on social-media platforms to sit alongside the work of journalists and the public statements of public figures, we gain nothing but volume and plurality; these are real and meaningful gains, to be sure, but they come with costs in attention and vulnerability, and they don't really bring us any closer to a forum for rational social and political consensus, if such a thing is even possible.

The second reason for putting my bluffer's broken heart on my sleeve is that this book will undoubtedly have readers who know more, and have more to say, about some or all of its subject matter than I do. I know some of the candidates already, in the academy and in the media and in the realm of political organising and activism, and have done my best in the time and space available to incorporate their published and private in-sights into this work. But there are worlds and lifetimes of experience and knowledge out there that I don't know and haven't touched. So, for all the doubts that I raise about the public sphere, this book is nonetheless an open invitation to a purposeful discussion about how to make better media and better politics; and I will try not to be embarrassed when confronted by wise friends and new acquaintances bearing the gift of 'I see you were writing about the public sphere ...'.

Over the course of 2016 and early 2017, as I researched this volume, friends and acquaintances had three public-sphere, media-related topics that they were most likely to hit me with: the treatment of the left parties, and especially Sinn Féin, in the general election of February 2016; the scandal that erupted around attempts to smear a whistleblower, Garda Sergeant Maurice McCabe, in early 2017;[1] and, of course, the mediated politics of an internationally resurgent nationalist right, a phenomenon that we might have dubbed 'Brexit' or 'Le Pen' until the US election in November 2016 gave us a perfectly, scarily satisfying one-syllable summary: 'Trump'.

The appalling McCabe case raises familiar questions about the persistence of unpublished gossip in Irish society, and the role of journalists in spreading it in a sort of sub-public (or public house) sphere. In 1979, for example, President Patrick Hillery felt he had to publicly deny that he had an extramarital relationship, even though not a word had been printed in the Irish media about the allegation. Although sources usually give stories to reporters in order to see them published, this is by no means always the case, especially if the story is so potentially defamatory that it could get a publisher in trouble. Often such stories are simply lubricants informing relationships of trust. I recall being at a public event where a senior politician said about a favoured journalist: 'I could tell him something and I knew I wouldn't have to worry about seeing it in the newspaper the next day.' Both men seemed to regard this as a compliment. In the McCabe case, it appears that crime correspondents were fed a malicious tale by Garda sources who expected that it would plant doubt about the whistleblower's credibility – doubts that the crime reporters brought back to their newsrooms, where other reporters were discouraged from taking up McCabe's 'tainted' allegations against the police force. The idea that this whispering campaign should itself have been the object of journalistic investigation was presumably too close to home for journalists accustomed to trading in whispers.

The 2016 election in the Republic highlighted a more ideological aspect of journalists' closeness to power. Political journalists largely adopted the outgoing government's line about the need for 'stability' in the context of recovery. As I wrote in *Village* magazine at the time (14 March 2016): 'Probably the greatest lines ever written about imperial, imperious government were those of Tacitus, speaking of the mighty Romans: "They made a desert, and called it peace".' Fine Gael, Labour and their media supporters 'gazed out over a wasteland they helped create, a desert of suicide, emigration, homelessness, overcrowded hospitals and regressive taxation to pay for it all, and they called it "stability".' Labour, most decisively punished by the electorate, accordingly won the most sympathy from pundits. As I wrote: 'Interviewers were busy before and after the election asking [Labour leader Joan Burton] and every other Labour politician: "To what do you attribute the people's ingratitude for your great achievements?" The answers generally admitted to "some shortcomings communicating to voters about our great achievements, perhaps because of our extraordinary dedication to achieving them".'

Before the vote, however, it was the treatment of Sinn Féin in the *Irish Independent* that was most striking. Day after day, the paper devoted page one to denouncing the party. In my view, however, this did at least as much to discredit the paper as the party; in today's media environment, more people probably saw social-media posts complaining about the *Independent*'s bias than actually paid for a copy of the newspaper. Like other Irish newspapers, the *Independent*'s circulation has fallen about forty per cent over the last decade. However, one should not take too much comfort from this evidence of falling media influence. When *Independent* journalist Paul Williams – himself a player in the McCabe events – went on RTÉ's *Late Late Show* days before the election to associate Sinn Féin with criminality, it not only raised questions about the broadcaster's duty to be balanced and impartial in election season, it *may* have been consequential for the election outcome. (Political scientists and historians are divided about media getting the credit, or blame, for electoral events, 'It was the *Sun* wot won it' style. The rise of the Labour Party in early twentieth-century Britain, for example, corresponded with some of the greatest concentration of media power ever seen, in the hands of a few right-wing 'press barons', not exactly an endorsement of the barons' power.)

And then there's Trump. Throughout 2016 and into 2017, Trump-watching provided material for any number of media-studies courses. Early on, as news networks showed his speeches and rallies, there was concern over the enormous amount of 'free' airtime he got, valued in the billions of dollars in various estimates. (The Democratic Party's left-wing insurgent, Bernie Sanders, was holding rallies of equal size and enthusiasm while getting less than one per cent of Trump's coverage.) Then, as Trump secured the Republican nomination, there was a period of media breast-beating, soon to be drowned out by an explosion of high-minded 'fact-checking'. By early 2017, Trump advisor Steve Bannon was referring to the media as 'the opposition'.

Alongside the media's evolution from Trump's facilitator to his enemy, arguments raged about assessing the balance of material and cultural reasons for his popularity. The world discovered the alt-right movement(s), presumed (with little evidence) to provide the online infrastructure for Trumpism. The nature and strategy for an online and offline culture of resistance to Trump were debated with ferocity. At least one thing seemed certain: culture was a political battleground, and though Trump's opponents dominated culture's traditional heights (Hollywood, most TV networks and major newspapers, the music and tech industries), it seemed that perhaps those heights had either been levelled, or got lost in the clouds.

Our media systems, many scholars argue, have moved from an economics of information to an economics of attention, whereby getting us to look, to click, is the constant and central objective. Donald Trump got our attention, all over the world, like perhaps no one has ever done before. Ironically, for all that he is a symptom of democratic and media decay, he is also the nearest thing we have had to a centre point for a global public sphere.

In the following pages I have organised my critical considerations of the public sphere, contingent and borrowed[2] as they may be, into three sections. The first, 'Bouncing the Sphere', introduces the public sphere as an historic idea and ideal, a place where proto-democratic and even truly democratic subjects deliberate and ensure civil society has a voice at the table of state. It challenges that idea in terms of its theoretical limitations and elisions and its ultimately technocratic-consensual model of how politics works, its evasion of 'the ineradicability of antagonism'. Jürgen Habermas, whose conception of the public sphere is at the root of most discussion of the subject, is a truly brilliant historian, philosopher and political observer, but this section suggests that the public sphere he spawned has nonetheless become an elusive object – one that is more useful for obscuring the realities of communicative political power behind a veil of liberal idealism than for revealing or, better yet, altering them for radical democratic purposes. Moreover, and whatever the merits of various efforts by Habermas and others to rescue the idea and make it relevant, the shattering of representative democracy in Europe and elsewhere in this century makes 'repairing the public sphere' even more of a distraction from the urgent task of fighting incipient political chaos, at best, and fascism, at worst.

Although Section 1 seeks in many respects to dispose of the concept of the public-sphere in theoretical terms, of course it doesn't fall so easily! Ultimately, as I concede in later sections, the public-sphere concept may in some specific cases be a useful 'distraction' in strategic terms for radical media activists: there may be instances where appeals to the value of the public sphere, and to journalists' high-minded self-regard, are politically necessary. Such an intellectual arabesque, both questioning and using a concept, is not uncommon when you seek to combine critique and activism. Indeed, criticism of media practice often gains impact when we measure it against (questionable) norms, such as the public sphere and journalistic professionalism. Insofar as the public sphere remains extant as a shorthand for the printed and electronic media systems where information is transmitted and exchanged, Sections 2 and 3 turn to a more detailed critique of their functioning in reality, with a particular focus on Irish examples. The first part of this turn from critiquing theory to critiquing practice is Section 2, 'Choking Off Circulation'. This section examines, among other things, what we can and can't learn by looking at media behaviour through the lens of its proprietors' commercial interests.

The biases of broadcasters and newspapers in the recent economic crisis are considered, along with the pressures and consequences of declining print circulation and migration of advertising online, as well as some initial questions about pluralism and the continuing important role of the public-service media, in Ireland and elsewhere. This section includes an extensive review of previously unpublished results of a study into newspaper coverage of the Irish movement against the Iraq War. While the Irish anti-war movement of 2002–03 is already relatively ancient history, its successes, failures and media profile remain highly relevant, given the continuing military use of Shannon airport and what may yet emerge as a renewed resistance to American imperialism, here and abroad.

Section 3, 'Likes, Shares And Leaves', moves the discussion online, where, though nearly infinite pluralism appears to rule the day, power and freedom are more elusive. Under the regime of what Jodi Dean calls 'communicative capitalism', in which the flow of information is itself commodified, we are all 'content providers', generally without remuneration – unless we are lucky enough to be bestowed with the neological title of 'social influencers'. For the rest of us, even our most politically radical postings and messages act as grist to the social-media-profiteers' mill, and as fodder for 'psychometric' experimentation for the purposes of political and commercial manipulation. Building on Dean's concept, the section explores how the continuing centrality of advertising and corporate power in digital media underlines the need to keep our eyes on the money, even when talking about a networked information environment. The familiar question of whether online engagement acts as a substitute for 'real world' politics is supplemented, in this section, with an examination of the 'real' content of virtual politics, and of whether we can explain some of the weirdest recent turns in the global political journey in light of special features of the online world, such as the 'fake news' that is widely supposed to have elected Donald Trump.

Finally, we look at media alternatives, if any, to the corporate control of potentially transformative communications. I regard the concept of the public sphere as hopelessly inadequate, at best. However, I believe that closely scrutinising its assumptions, strategically considering its uses, and exploring other ways of understanding and producing information about public life are precisely the sort of activities that media-conscious activists should engage in. These conceptual actions, embodied in this book, constitute (I like to think) the erection of some small signposts on the road to Utopia. In keeping with the theme of the Síreacht series, I hope they encourage readers to imagine a healthier environment for public communication in the context of a better Ireland and a better world.

Bouncing the Sphere

It's one of those metaphors – like a hat in the ring or shit hitting the fan – that has long since transcended its metaphorical status. It requires no pause to consider, no mental image, to unearth its meaning. Indeed, most of the time it's used, its meaning is banal and the recourse to the phrase is gratuitous. When some pontificator tells us that some piece of information is 'in the public sphere' or even 'circulating in the public sphere', it's rarely to add any significance that the word 'public' would fail to achieve on its own steam.

Sometimes we find the phrase 'public sphere' is tinged with regret or even distaste, the emphasis on 'public' contrasting with what might be more appropriately regarded as private: did some entertainer's widely rumoured extramarital affair, for example, really belong 'in the *public* sphere' – meaning, generally, a tabloid newspaper? More often, though, the 'public sphere' is ringed, Saturn-like, with a halo of virtue, so that a *Guardian* opinion article about the use of legal preventative measures to keep those very same sexual shenanigans out of those very same newspapers is headlined 'Injunctions protect the public sphere'.[3] In this formulation, the sphere seems to have a purity of shape and of composition that is sadly distorted when inappropriate and unwarranted material seeks to find refuge under its surface.

This section will consider how this apparently banal but somehow sanctified little object has been developed intellectually as both an historic and contemporary account of the communicative relations between citizens and state. Looking at the way the term's late-twentieth-century adoption coincides with a 'high modernist' conception of journalism's positive role in society, I will raise questions about the theoretical and political application of such idealisations. Perhaps tossing around the public sphere is a misleading distraction from a more accurate understanding of the forces that stand in ineradicable opposition in capitalist society, whether they appear to be 'debating' each other or not.

But it is such a simple and attractive metaphor. When we start to think about the public sphere more carefully and when we consider what the metaphor might contribute to meaning, it becomes associated with a sort of pleasing rotundity, a sense of proportion and circularity that may remind us of our planet, or of our favourite sport. When I walk into a classroom where a colleague has recently been teaching undergraduate students about it, I can usually expect to see the public sphere represented on the whiteboard as a circle, often with curved arrows of information, opinion, deliberation and exchange spinning around its interior in two or three marker colours – blue for the politicians, red for the interest groups, green for the general population – in a picture that looks very dynamic yet well balanced.

The sense of circularity that attends the idea of public sphere is something of an accident of translation. The German title of Jürgen Habermas' 1962 book, finally published in English twenty-seven years later as *The Structural Transformation of the Public Sphere*, mentioned nothing spherical; indeed, there was no mention of any object, solid or metaphorical, of any shape at all. The word Habermas used was *Öffentlichkeit*, which needless to say is difficult to translate, but if you were being literal, you'd just use 'public' as a noun, given that 'publicity' is already taken by another vernacular definition, and 'publicness' errs on the insubstantial side. The public thing that Habermas wants us to consider has real material dimensions, and sphere helps us get there. (The translation of the subtitle, *An Inquiry into a Category of Bourgeois Society*, throws up further complications, but since Habermas himself gave his blessing to the translation, we cannot regard either 'public sphere' or 'bourgeois' as being in some way contrary to the author's intention.)

Even in English, of course, a 'sphere' is not necessarily a ball, despite the Greek and Latin roots that say it is. The blogosphere needn't be especially round, nor is the private sphere necessarily seen as a realm of metaphorical circulation. Sphere can just mean an area or aspect of activity. However, the public sphere, for better or worse, tends to want to take on a circular form. You only need look at the image that, as of late 2017, illustrates the Wikipedia page 'Public sphere': in an apparently old black-and-white photograph, several men, mostly wearing turbans, are sitting in a rough circle.[4] The caption tells us it's 'A coffeehouse discussion'. Indeed, Habermas himself cites the eighteenth-century European coffeehouse and the discussions that took place there as his sort of ideal form of *Öffentlichkeit*. Funny, though, that this image is evidently neither European (the brown-skinned turbaned men) nor eighteenth century (it's a photo!). If we look at the image selected by the Wikipedia 'hive mind' (the collective intelligence of its users) to illuminate the concept more closely, and click through the image's links to learn more about its history, some of the complications of thinking of the public sphere as a space for the equal and deliberate exchange of ideas of political significance come into clearer focus.

For one thing, there are only men in this highly gendered sphere. Secondly, the men do not appear to be of equal standing: most of them are white-bearded and drink coffee, but, nearer the camera, younger men, also seated, are involved in making and serving the coffee – are they part of the sphere? Click further and find out that the image was uploaded to Wikimedia in 2004 by a trusted US-based user named 'Infrogmation', who scanned it from 'a period stereoscope card in my possession'. Uncropped, it includes a caption: 'A Coffee-house in Palestine'. The photograph dates from the early twentieth century, and in this form is a piece of exotica aimed at an American audience, showing men in a land that, in fact, has virtually no political autonomy under Ottoman imperial rule – a rule that would soon be replaced by British and then Israeli dominion. A 1913 caption for the image found elsewhere online is labelled as coming from the 'Keystone View Company' – a company that specialised in selling Americans various scenic images of natives from around the world – and the long caption tells us that the men 'converse with each other, and tell stories, the delight of the Arab sheik'; none of the men in the image, however, appears to be speaking. Now these silent men, photographed more than a century ago facing the orientalist gaze, are memorialised as somehow exemplary of the 'public sphere' on Wikipedia, the collaborative encyclopedia that is the twenty-first century's own idealised version of a public space devoted to the equality of all contributors and the rational pursuit of truth.

The discrepancy between image and reality is central to trying to understand what's helpful about the concept of the public sphere and what, on the other hand, is distracting and misleading. The fact, for example, that a particular 'public' that may have access to a given public sphere does not constitute an entire population doesn't mean the sphere is not public, just that it is not fully democratic or representative, a problem to which we will return. If one visits the excavated remains of the ancient agora (marketplace) in Athens, it is important to understand that the Athenian democracy reflected in its ruins and relics was hugely limited, practically and morally, being only for people who were male, free, adult and citizens (less than twenty per cent of the population, which contained a huge number of slaves and a not-quite-so-huge number of foreigners). But it is also important to recognise that its formal rituals and informal discussions, its machinery of elections, selections and ostracisms and its spaces for debate and decision-making constituted a set of ways of relating a population to its governance that makes the city-state's agora something like the original public sphere, notwithstanding its obvious limitations.

For Habermas, most of the years since the classical period were characterised by autocratic and feudal modes of life and governance that couldn't and didn't give rise to the distinctive mode of a-people-being-public that he calls a public sphere. When power emanates from and through the persona of the lord or king, when the state *is* him, then there is no potential connection between public discussion of current affairs and the practice of state and economic power, and therefore there is no public sphere. But all-powerful monarchies were largely overthrown or replaced. By the seventeenth and eighteenth centuries in north-west Europe, long before states there fully adopted and embraced the ancient language of 'democracy' to account for the relation of government and the people who are governed, there were structures and institutions for the development and transmission of public opinion that provided, says Habermas, a complex and responsive public sphere that linked the bourgeois world of commerce with the aristocratic/political realm of public affairs.

This public sphere could no longer be the single physical marketplace of an ancient city state, where a few thousand men might gather to decide public policy. Instead, the bourgeois public sphere was a more networked, less formal affair, the sum total of hundreds of coffeehouse conversations, where mercantile actors might discuss the policies and regulations that affected them. These conversations were now fuelled by the information gathered in the vital new bourgeois institution of the newspaper press, which had emerged most particularly in the busy trading environment of republican Amsterdam in the 1600s. As this version of public life developed, Enlightenment ideologues such as Thomas Jefferson went so far as to establish new republican forms of government that would be the living embodiment of the public sphere; Jefferson himself understood that the public sphere (though he was not using that term) was as important as the formal mechanisms of any nascent American democracy. He wrote: 'The basis of our governments being the opinion of the people, the very first object should be to keep that right; and were it left to me to decide whether we should have a government without newspapers or newspapers without a government, I should not hesitate a moment to prefer the latter.'[5]

Jefferson was as capable of hating newspapers as any other politician, and the feeling was mutual: he was a particular target of the press in the early US. Nonetheless, the relatively freewheeling public sphere of the new American republic, in the form of a press that produced not just newspapers but also a vibrant range of opinionated pamphlets, gave new, unprecedented space even to advocates of the rights of those excluded from most facets of public life, including women and slaves.

For Habermas, the point of the historic public sphere was not that, through it, the public made a claim to rule, in the form of democracy. In his original formulation, the question of formal institutions of democracy was something separate from the public sphere. The bourgeois public sphere of the eighteenth and nineteenth centuries was not in itself an electoral arena for selecting rulers, but instead subjected those who ruled to rational-critical debate that assessed them according to logic and law. And it wasn't just politics; Habermas quotes a wide-eyed contemporary who notes: 'after the world for millennia had gotten along quite well without it, in the middle of the eighteenth century all of a sudden art criticism bursts on the scene'.[6]

Two or three centuries later, we still have art criticism, and plenty of it, but do we still have a public sphere worth describing in those terms? Habermas, in his original study, didn't suggest that a true public sphere continued to exist in mid-twentieth-century democracies. Indeed, his 1962 book was partly understood as a lament for the disappearance of such a structure in the face of mass consumerism, among other forces, that made people grasping and privatistic rather than rational and civic-minded. Such an elegy echoed the disappointed politics of some of his predecessors in the famous Frankfurt School. Just as Adorno and Horkheimer regarded twentieth-century popular culture as mindless mass-produced baby food for the mind, Habermas suggested that by the twentieth century a rational public sphere had given way to a politics produced according to the distracting logic of advertising and public relations (PR), and a diverse print culture had given way to a corporate-dominated one.

But the story of the public sphere doesn't end with a 1962 historical study by a German political philosopher. If it did, we would be safe enough in describing the public sphere as an historical 'was', a communicative phenomenon that coincided with a particular phase in the social and technological history of capitalism. However, for Habermas in subsequent writings and for others who have picked up the idea, the public sphere has more than historical dimensions: it's not only a 'was', but an 'is', or it's at least a 'should be', tied up in a vision of how political communication facilitates the circulation of ideas in a more or less democratic society. In its most idealistic form, the public sphere encompasses a set of institutions and technologies – including some of the ones revealed by the ICT revolution of our century – that allow the population of a locality, region or country to deliberate on policy and politics, deliberations that can then feed into the formal processes of parliamentary democracy. This deliberating could take the form of anything from opinion polling to televised town-hall debates to social-media discussion threads.

In the rest of this book, then, we'll respectfully set aside the original Habermasian 'was' and concentrate our minds on the question of what the public sphere is, if indeed it is anything in 2018, and on the still larger question of whether the concept provides a useful model of what should be. Are the shortcomings in our democracies fundamentally related to deficiencies in what we choose to call the public sphere? I will argue, rather, that obsessing about problems in the public sphere – such the recent kerfuffle over 'fake news' – can act as a convenient excuse for ignoring the deeper structures of inequity and oppression in our societies. While it may be valuable in its own right to seek to make our media institutions and their output more inclusive, more scrupulous, more diverse, more responsive, it is highly unlikely to lead to significant improvements for the victims of those structures. We'll ask whether, and when, we might need to work to create and maintain some elements of a unitary public sphere – a powerful and popular public broadcaster, for example – while we also acknowledge that there are now separate, albeit occasionally intersecting, spheres (filter bubbles and silos appear to be the reigning metaphors), with one for leftists, another for conservatives, a feminist sphere where you rarely if ever see the contents of the misogynist sphere, a racist sphere untroubled by immigrants, etc. We'll even ask if 'debate' is all it's cracked up to be.

One fundamental problem with an idealised public sphere is the question of its irreducible individual subject: what kind of person should you be in the public sphere? Does a 'good' public sphere come with expectations about its good participants? American scholar Michael Schudson, drawing on TV cartoon comedy, suggests that the Habermasian public sphere has evolved a

'Lisa Simpson' model of its ideal member, an informed and curious citizen who combines adherence to certain basic liberal-democratic principles with a commitment to learning about issues in order to participate fully, thoughtfully, politely and conscientiously in debates.[7] This is the 'eat your vegetables' ideal of the good citizen, the character reflected back to us in the advertising for the better sort of newspapers: 'Before you make up your mind, open it', as the *Irish Independent* has lightly punned in its ad campaigns for many years. One problem, as Schudson points out, is that Lisa Simpson scarcely resembles the typical citizen of the public-sphere's Habermasian prime in the late eighteenth and early nineteenth centuries, when a man entered the public sphere more like Homer Simpson entering Moe's: because his mates were there and he fancied a drink. The public sphere was a ring where you went to join with your faction and to fight for it, not a book that you opened in order to make up your mind. (Any newspaper you opened in those days was almost certain to be highly partisan, untainted by later ideals of objectivity.)

If Schudson's Homeric sketch of the publicly spherical citizen of the past is something of a caricature, it seems to me that he is onto something when he suggests that a super-virtuous Lisa figure provides the (rather off-putting) ideal of the good citizen in the public sphere that we have inherited from the late twentieth century, a dry ideal that owes something to Habermas himself, as well as to the self-regard of certain key media institutions. Although it has, in the last few years, become a much more difficult fiction to maintain, the basic idea that our major media parked themselves beside our democratic governments to provide us with at least the opportunity to inhabit the best of all political worlds remains an influential one. In this version of the political-media universe, such failings of democracy as we have suffered are the consequence of a citizenry that, damn us, just won't eat our vegetables: we get the government and media we deserve, to use a familiar phrase.

Paper Tigers

Despite the evident failings and insistent triviality of the vast majority of the media output to which we are exposed, most of us remain in the shadow of a late-twentieth-century image that scholar Daniel Hallin calls the 'high modernism' of journalism.[8] This high modernism is not exactly the same as the idea, or ideal, of the public sphere, but the picture painted by the so-called modernists was hugely influential at a time when a simplified version of the vision of Habermas was disseminated widely, and the two ideas make a good fit. In fact, in my view, the history of the idea of the public sphere over the last half-century is inseparable from the high-modernist narcissism of journalists, their employers and (yes) those teaching and writing about journalism, who saw their roles reflected flatteringly in the theory. In other words, the public sphere became an idea, or set of ideas, about the important role played by the media in democratic societies at just the time that journalists most confidently cast themselves in such a role.

High modernism in journalism was, according to Hallin, a guiding ideology of the major newspapers and broadcasters of the US, but, like most other American cultural and ideological constructs, it travelled well. It's still to be found on many an 'about us' section of a newspaper website, or in the course documents of journalism programmes at colleges, universities and institutes throughout the world, and in various journalistic codes of conduct and practice. The achingly high-minded articles of association of the Irish Times Trust were signed in 1974, reflecting the absolute pinnacle of its influence. It's easy enough to describe the role of journalism as interpreted by such high modernism: intrepid journalists bravely report unbiased facts about serious public and political affairs without fear or favour, while also reporting and weighing up a range of opinions about the proper conduct of such affairs, and acting as vehicles for responsible public debate. By producing such reliable and rational knowledge about the world, they fulfil a social responsibility, promoting understanding and democracy and, ultimately, making the world a better place. Needless to say, even the most confident adherents of this model acknowledged that it didn't describe the actual history of journalism very well at all, nor did it encompass all contemporary journalistic practice; but it was seen, according to Hallin, not merely as the highest calling of journalistic practice, but as its obvious end point, the place where journalism found its final destiny.

The influence in the wider culture of this blindingly burnished image peaked in the mid-1970s, when two named reporters from the *Washington Post* were elevated to starring roles in the Watergate scandal that brought down President Nixon. Hollywood even got its two biggest stars, Robert Redford and Dustin Hoffman, to play those reporters, Bob Woodward and Carl Bernstein.

However, the reach of journalistic high modernism transcended Watergate, as the death early in 2017 of TV actor Mary Tyler Moore reminded us. You see, Moore was responsible for perhaps the oddest output of that cultural moment when journalism was at its ideological height. Beginning in 1970, Moore produced and starred in a half-hour sitcom focusing on a young woman's life in a TV newsroom, which was depicted with light satire: the vain, empty-headed anchorman, the wise-cracking writer, the irascible boss, and so on. But in 1977, for the first and only time in US TV history, that half-hour comedy series 'spun off' a one-hour drama series. The grumpy boss, played by Ed Asner, became the eponymous city editor of a big newspaper in *Lou Grant*, but now, with the modernist wind blowing from the direction of Watergate, satire was nowhere to be seen. The new show was a permanently earnest, if occasionally funny, newspaper procedural. For the five years that it ran as one of CBS's top-rated programmes, there could be little doubt that Lou and the intrepid young reporters he mentored were doing God's work in trying to shed light on their town, Los Angeles, with only the lightest of interference from a pleasingly pliant, amusingly patrician matriarchal publisher. Two decades ahead of *The West Wing* in its loving portrait of conscientious liberals wielding great power responsibly, *Lou Grant* was the high modernism of US journalism in weekly dramatic action. I cannot have been the only teenager who watched and was hooked by the allure of the press card, which seemed a licence to do the most socially and morally uplifting work in the world while you remained pleasingly rough around the edges, even irascible. (By comparison, the 2015 film *Spotlight*, about the *Boston Globe* investigation of clerical sex abuse, was positively grimy in its acknowledgment of journalists' capacity to fail, and its Oscar success – despite merely fair-to-middling box office – surely reflected a certain nostalgia for the glorious 1970s of heroic journalistic tales.)

There are plenty of problems with the high-modernist vision as it relates to the 1970s, problems we needn't go into here. However, there was already a widespread consensus by the early 1990s, before the Internet became central to journalism's fate, that the golden age, such as it was, seemed to be over. Hallin's own article on 'the passing' of high modernism was published in 1992. American journalist-scholar Doug Underwood published a book the following year that lamented the takeover of newspapers by money-hungry corporations, and more books from both sides of the Atlantic went on to date the start of the rot to the 1980s, long before dotcoms bubbled and burst.[9] All of the research pointed to changes in workplace organisation that meant those TV-drama reporters who could spend weeks working on a story had largely become a thing of the past; journalists were expected to churn out product just like the next cog in the corporate machine. Thus, complex investigations could rarely be done, and publishing or broadcasting lightly edited PR bumf from governments, companies and other special interests generally represented the shortest distance through an overwhelming journalistic workday. We'll look at specific features of media content and practice, especially in Ireland, in Section 2, but it's worth noting here that there has also been a perceptible 'genre shift' in the balance of journalism produced throughout the Western world over the last three decades. Before Donald Trump became box-office gold, there was a distinct turning away from public and political affairs as the dominant content of most news outlets. For example, Hallin cites 'increased personalisation' in media, a focus 'on "private" life and on individual experience'. This 'depoliticisation', he says, means 'a shrinking away of the public sphere which increases the power of elites by leaving important areas of social life outside the arena of public debate'.[10]

This analysis is fine as far as it goes. But it tends to locate the 'shrinking of the [alleged] public sphere' as a media-centred problem, one closely related to the declining autonomy of journalists within their working field; that declining autonomy results in shrinking space for the traditional values of objectivity and public service within their practice, now seen to be dominated by corporate bosses who love nothing more than retreads of celebrity fluff. What if we view the problem through a wider lens?

Perhaps we should pull back from the media per se and look at how journalism interacts with the political realm, in a highly sophisticated cyclical interplay of mutual dependency. British scholar Nick Couldry sees the media as complicit partners in a neoliberal and technocratic depoliticisation of politics itself: 'What if the workings of the media/political cycle themselves, far from increasing politics' accountability via media to voters, favour a shift away from political deliberation ...?' Couldry answers his own question in the affirmative: 'the symbiosis of mainstream media and neoliberal government appears to strengthen the tendency for government mandates or policy directives to operate below the level of normative debate', he writes, with the possibility that the 'loss of a wider deliberative language for politics may be neoliberal democracy's most far-reaching legacy'.[11] In a variation on the theme of how contemporary statecraft has increasingly removed certain vast and important topics from the sphere of public discussion and deliberation, critical theorist Giorgio Agamben writes that the 'atomic age has increased the perimeter of state secrecy and raison d'etat, in which, for example, atomic plants are shrouded, restricting the perimeter of the public sphere accordingly'.[12]

If, by the late twentieth century, ever-dumber media were joining forces with ever-more-technocratic-and-secretive government to shrink the public sphere and reduce both our capacity for, and the subject-matter of, political deliberation, did the twenty-first-century explosion of digital communication make things even worse? That's a matter of considerable debate, some of which we'll return to in the final section. For now, it's worth noting that these days for every cyber-optimist, there are two other people arguing that online politics is a tragedy for the public sphere because we don't hear 'the other side' and lack common media experiences upon which we can deliberate rationally as societies. A characteristic handwringing editorial in the *Economist* lamented that 'Facebook, Google and Twitter were supposed to save politics [!] as good information drove out prejudice and falsehood', but that things have gone badly wrong and through their algorithms they in fact 'threaten democracy'.[13] In this vision of a lost communal public sphere, we find ourselves apologetically claiming that, no, we're not completely blinkered, there's a cousin of ours on Facebook who seems to have voted for Trump.

Beyond Lamentation

In much of this media and academic agonising about a public sphere that shrinks, becomes opaque or is at risk of shattering, there is an unavoidable sense that we need urgent action to reinflate it, clean up its surface, or otherwise preserve and protect it; that a new politics could somehow emerge in all its glory if only we could all get into that sphere and, God help us, deliberate properly.

But what if all this lamentation, despite the lamenters' sincere hand-wringing and genuine desire for reform, is a mark of misplaced faith in the institutions of Western governance? What if, in our eagerness to restore or create a rich and pluralist public sphere, we're letting those institutions, in the utter hollowness of their capacity to deliver anything like popular sovereignty, completely off the hook? Aren't earnest and angry debates about 'fake news' mere trivial distractions from the urgent action that is needed to address our 'fake democracies'?

Whatever Habermas' original intentions, it is arguable that he and his ideas of the public sphere and deliberative democracy have now done more to cloak the realities of the capitalist-controlled institutions that govern us than to shed light upon them. Habermas himself has, unfortunately, become something of a source of confusion. On the one hand, he freely admits that neoliberalism has closed down the range of possibilities for political action and for a genuine public sphere to guide it. He acknowledges how far we are from deliberative democracy, but, on the other hand, as Deborah Cook writes of one of his 1990s books, he advances a 'more conciliatory' position:

> Acknowledging the defects in current political practices, procedures and institutions, [Habermas] nonetheless judges these states to be 'more or less' – a recurring phrase – democratic, in the stronger, ideal sense of that term. He thereby effectively collapses the distinction that he himself has set up between an ideal, constitutionally regulated polity and its instantiation in existing liberal democracies.[14]

In more recent times, since the crisis of 2007–08 and its ugly aftermath, he has argued strongly for a strengthening of EU institutions, with the engagement of transnational civil-society institutions – the rising, in effect, of a European public sphere out of the ashes of the EU's crushing of democratic ambitions in Greece and elsewhere. If this seems an unlikely form of resurrection, the capacity of Habermas to envision it, despite all his criticisms, has positioned him as a defender of Angela Merkel and the push to further empower the European, and euro, core.[15] The German philosopher's willingness, indeed eagerness, to kick the centre of rational deliberation ever upward into higher supranational structures – in part as a means of neutralising and undermining the clear and present danger of renascent nationalism – has ended up looking more like a defence of neoliberal technocrats than a way of defeating them.

The reality of those EU institutions, and the risks of viewing them through a Habermasian lens, were captured in an article by Greek intellectual and activist Stathis Kouvelakis, himself formerly part of the leadership of Greece's left-wing Syriza party. His Greek comrades, he said, were not ready to fight against the EU–IMF–European Central Bank troika in the spring and summer of 2015 precisely because they believed they could reason with them. The Greek minister for finance, Euclid Tsakalotos, had told a French journalist how disappointed he was to find that at a Brussels ministerial meeting, despite the detailed and (he thought) persuasive paper he had delivered in advance to EU colleagues,

there was a low level of debate. 'The other finance min-
isters just recited rules and procedures!' he complained.
Tsakalotos, according to Kouvelakis, 'was living in some
kind of Habermasian dreamworld, presupposing a will
to find common ground, a "win-win deal"'. Ultimately,
writes Kouvelakis, Syriza 'lacked not just the perception
of class antagonism but the elementary realism that any
political figure needs in order to survive'.[16]

This, then, is the more fundamental critique of the
idea of the public sphere: it lures us into a false sense that
politics is a matter of debate and persuasion, of rational
deliberation and perhaps even consensus, rather than a
realm of unavoidably competing interests. It seems to
me that a much more useful way to consider how politics
play out, and how their ideological range is restricted in
ways that serve the status quo, is through the concept
of 'hegemony'. This idea, most richly developed by the
Italian Marxist Antonio Gramsci, and by many
Gramscians, neo-Gramscians and assorted revisers,
theorises how certain groups, and the ideas that support
them, achieve and maintain political and cultural
'leadership' in society. Attentiveness to the process
of hegemony means that you can't begin to discuss
political ideas without consideration of how they relate
to structures of real, material power. Hegemony doesn't
mean that the powerful are a monolithic bloc or that
no challenging ideas ever reach the media; indeed,
successful hegemony is often based on the tolerance
and absorption of potential opposition rather than the
crushing of it.[17] But an understanding of hegemony

means that it's very difficult to believe, even in theory, in a public sphere where ideas compete equally for implementation.

Some of the most sophisticated Gramscian attacks on the major liberal conception of the public sphere, with its ultimately technocratic sense that decisions can be rationally made on the basis of what works best for society at large, have come from the writings of Chantal Mouffe and Ernesto Laclau. Writing together, the Belgian and Argentine scholars insist on the usefulness of hegemony to 'help us to understand that the present conjuncture, far from being the only natural or possible societal order, is the expression of a certain configuration of power relations'. They continue: 'It is the result of hegemonic moves on the part of specific social forces which have been able to implement a profound transformation in the relations between capitalist corporations and the nation-states.' In order to challenge the power of those forces, they explain, it's necessary to break from the idea that we share a defined and stable 'public sphere' with them; it 'requires drawing new political frontiers and acknowledging that there cannot be a radical politics without the definition of an adversary. That is to say, it requires the acceptance of the ineradicability of antagonism.'[18]

As 'post-Marxists', Mouffe and Laclau are not inclined to reduce the basic social antagonism to one defined by class. Indeed, part of their mission has been to advocate for potentially revolutionary alliances that join up diverse groups of the marginalised, exploited and oppressed into a potential new hegemonic bloc – one that would, even if successful, never actually eradicate all potential antagonisms. The centrality of antagonism, they write, 'forecloses any possibility of a final reconciliation, of any kind of rational consensus, of a fully inclusive we. For us, a non-exclusive public sphere of rational argument is a conceptual impossibility.'[19] They continue:

> This is why we stress that it is vital for democratic politics to acknowledge that any form of consensus is the result of a hegemonic articulation, and that it always has an 'outside' that impedes its full realization. Unlike the Habermasians, we do not see this as something that undermines the democratic project, but as its very condition of possibility.[20]

This basic idea – to hell with rationality and harmony, it's not how we roll – should ultimately be liberating. Indeed, it may be coming into its own, as 'progressive' people who thought it was possible to engage deliberatively with the neoliberal forces of the Clinton–Blair era that gave rise to Laclau and Mouffe's rejection now find themselves face to face with people and forces that themselves openly reject most forms of consensus and rationality. It is far easier, in 2018, to see our political and class enemies as 'ineradicably antagonistic'.

Even before Trump, however, the mask had slipped. In Ireland and elsewhere in the European periphery, economic catastrophes that were not of our making were laid at our doorsteps, at the ever-increasing cost of inequality and collapsing public services. As Mouffe has written more recently: 'The role of parliaments and institutions that allow citizens to influence policy decisions was drastically reduced'. Many of our states, as Wolfgang Streeck writes, are reduced to 'debt-collecting agencies on behalf of a global oligarchy of investors'.[21] So much for 'the power of people', even through their elected representatives. Governments either explicitly or implicitly constituted and guided by technocrats, presiding over growing inequality, have become the order of the day. Mouffe notes that the most basic understanding of democracy has been abandoned and all that is left is a shell: 'Today, talking about "democracy" is only to refer to the existence of elections and the defense of human rights.'[22] It should go without saying (but perhaps it doesn't) that being able to vote to change the camera-fronting personnel of government, but not its policies, scarcely qualifies as rule by the demos.[23]

What this understanding of our existing democracies underlines is that the mere presence of disagreement does not a functional public sphere make. To put it more simply: what if you're constantly arguing but the same people always quietly win? As media scholar Natalie Fenton puts it: 'equating a healthy democracy with a multiplicity of counter-publicity would appear severely misplaced'. One human right, the defence of which Mouffe regards as among the last residues of our democracies is, after all, free speech. So with the capacity to voice dissenting views largely (though far from completely) protected, we can congratulate ourselves on the vigorous pluralism of our politics. As Fenton writes: 'It is deemed to be enough simply to display a supermarket of views and perspectives and so present an illusion of political choice.'[24] In reality, you and your pals can deliberate all you like on the widest conceivable range of politics; on the fundamentals of how the economy and society are organised, your conclusions are entirely irrelevant to how things will continue to work. States themselves have less and less room to deliberate relevantly, as Fenton writes: 'As supranational organizations such as the IMF and the WTO are not accountable to the public, it is hardly surprising that successive and global protests against the WTO have met with a deafening silence.'[25]

The illusion fostered by powerless pluralism is indeed most stark, and most poignant, when people take to the streets in their thousands and millions to oppose the policies of supranational or even national institutions. It would be wrong to say that large popular mobilisations never have an effect on policy; the Irish state's fudges on the question of the Irish Water utility, for example, demonstrate that governments have to watch out for popular opinion on the margins and in their messaging, if only to ensure that they themselves remain the personnel assigned to serve the needs of neoliberal governance, rather than being replaced at an election by some alternative parliamentary bloc. However, the reality is that public demonstrations rarely change policy. We need only consider the largest worldwide mobilisation against a specific political prospect ever, on the eve of the US invasion of Iraq. In the immediate aftermath of the millions who marched in February 2003, a *New York Times* analyst was famously moved to remark that there appeared to be 'two super-powers on the planet: the United States and world public opinion' (17 February 2003). Ten years on, a writer in *Time* magazine was still agonising about why such a move-ment went unheeded.[26] One of the 'superpowers', the real one, carried on with its illegal invasion of a sovereign country with scarcely a thought about public opinion – its leader being re-elected the following year – while the other alleged superpower quietly vanished from the scene.

This is not to say that political demonstrations are necessarily pointless, a waste of time, or a minor act of political conscience-laundering for participants – though they may indeed qualify sometimes as any or all of those things. It's simply to observe that the existence of occasional political outrage and turmoil as a public spectacle scarcely points to the existence of a genuine-ly contentious and deliberative public sphere in which such actions, and the ideas that animate them, contrib-ute meaningfully to the formation of policy. As the late, great John Berger wrote in 1968: 'Theoretically demon-strations are meant to reveal the strength of popular opinion or feeling: theoretically they are an appeal to the democratic conscience of the State. But this presupposes a conscience which is very unlikely to exist.'[27] It might be argued that Berger was writing in the midst of an inter-national movement against the Vietnam War, a move-ment that by some accounts was ultimately successful.

A more dispassionate analysis would, however, have to concede that dissent within the ranks of the US forces and military resistance in the invaded nation(s) were far more important factors in the US defeat in South East Asia. The latter factor, armed fightback, has of course been more influential over the last fifteen years of American struggle in the 'global war on terror' than any 'public sphere' protests have been.

Demonstrations, especially in large-scale ongoing campaigns, may indeed be framed as publicly spherical appeals to democratic conscience. But the fact that they are taking place at all provides some evidence of the absence of such conscience. As Berger writes: 'If the State authority is open to democratic influence, the demonstration will hardly be necessary; if it is not, it is unlikely to be influenced by an empty show of force containing no real threat.' So why demonstrate at all? For Berger the answer is simple: to rehearse for revolution. 'The delay between the rehearsals and the real performance may be very long: their quality – the intensity of rehearsed awareness – may, on different occasions, vary considerably', he writes, 'but any demon-stration which lacks this element of rehearsal is better described as an officially encouraged public spectacle.'[28]

Of course a great many demonstrations – though arguably not enough – refute any accusation of being mere 'officially encouraged public spectacles' by virtue of their illegality. Whether it's sitting down in a road, burning a limousine or punching a Nazi, there are a range of actions that, whatever their efficacy, certainly put the actors at some risk and more directly challenge the idea of the rational, deliberative and wholly legal public sphere. It is no accident, therefore, that these are the actions most likely to arouse the ire of the media, the embodiment of that sphere. Before one demonstration at Shannon airport in the early days of the Iraq War, I wrote an article for the *Irish Times* explaining why the action was necessary, and why we protesters were prepared to sit down and block traffic for a short time to make a point about the horrors being facilitated through an Irish civilian airport. Despite my invocations of Nuremberg, Thoreau and King in defence of civil disobedience, the opinion editor at that respected liberal newspaper wrote to me explaining that he was retracting his earlier 'hasty acceptance' of my offer of an article: the paper now realised it should not be 'associated with and assist in mobilising for a call to break the law – a step too far!'[29]

In Ireland, the likes of Occupy Dame Street (part of a vital global movement of dubious legality in 2011–12), the #HomeSweetHome initiative to house homeless people by taking over Dublin's NAMA-owned Apollo House, and the many trespass-based anti-war actions at Shannon that have occurred over the last fifteen years point not to some thriving public sphere but to its absence; activity at the fringes of the law, away from would-be deliberative institutions of media or legislation, becomes necessary to secure public attention or socio-political ends. As Deborah Cook writes: 'Such radical forms of political expression would surely not be required if Western states were routinely as responsive to the concerns of citizens as Habermas occasionally declares they ought to be.'[30]

We'll look more closely at how journalists, and especially Irish journalists, consistently police the limits of public debate in the next section. In Section 3, which focuses on the Internet as a communicative sphere, we'll consider whether the undoubtedly genuine, albeit limited, pluralism to be found online means that we can and should talk meaningfully about public spheres in the plural. For now, it is vital that we understand how the central idea of the unitary public sphere has been damaged, both in theory and in practice, by its own limits as an historical and contemporary construct and by the destructive power of neoliberal capitalism and the states and international bodies that sustain it. The public sphere, I have tried to argue, is at best an anachronism and at worst a lie that facilitates a deadly, repressive and unequal status quo, a lie that only media outlets and mainstream politicians have any real interest in repeating.

But wait, a reader might object: isn't there a danger of throwing out the baby (reasoned, constructive debate) with the bathwater (the public sphere)? To which my first, instinctive reply would be: let the baby go – it doesn't belong to us either. This response is, of course, an oversimplification; in the following sections I may indeed concede that the bathwater can be splashed around strategically to some cleansing effect. As for the baby – perhaps we can enjoy playing with it without believing it's going to grow up to change the world, be it as Rosa Parks, Martin Luther King or even Beyoncé.

Debate can of course be useful, and indeed fun. But any real positive function of getting involved in public debate – for example, as a sort of performance of political credibility that may be valuable for people advancing unusual or challenging ideas – should not be allowed to get mixed up with a liberal public-sphere notion that we debate as part of a deliberative democratic process that will result in rational consensus. For most liberals, 'healthy debate' is a good in itself and a vital constituent of the public sphere. For radicals who understand something about hegemony, it's overrated. And sometimes it's worse than overrated: for example, the fine Irish scholar of migration and racial politics, Gavan Titley, has written powerfully of how the insistence that we 'shouldn't be afraid to debate' the role of immigrants in society is used to cover racism. Titley writes: 'antiracist scholars, in a context now of conflict and markedly racializing politics, have to examine the ways in which the public denial and deflection of racism is being secured not just through silencing, but through debatability.'[31]

This critique of debate does not, or at least should not, mean that we hesitate to engage with ideas. It just means that we do so cognisant of the relations of power in which they are situated. We critique 'debatability' not because we are certain that we are right or because we are afraid that we will be proven wrong, but because we understand that the genuine challenges to hegemonic power must be built outside that hegemony – close to it, sure, but not under its wing, where it sets the terms of debate. And we build that counter-hegemony not by ignoring difference – we plunge right into it, dialectically building our ideas in the conflicts that arise, not pretending that we can produce rational compromises with those whose interests fundamentally differ from our own, in some magical public sphere.

Whenever I hear about the wonders of 'debate', I think of Chelsea Manning. In the face of seven years of psychoanalysing what brought her to leak classified US documents to Wikileaks, she has had one consistent line about her motivation, repeated at her pre-trial hearing: she wished to 'spark a domestic debate on the role of the military and our foreign policy'.[32] Instead, while the mediated 'public sphere' was happy to use many of her revelations, the main debate it entertained was about her sanity. It's better, I suppose, that the information she revealed about American military and diplomatic wrongdoing was made public than that it should remain secret; I myself have written journalistic stories based on the Wikileaks documents, so I've got an interest in believing that. But the cost for Manning – imprisoned, tortured, driven to suicide attempts, and thankfully now free – has been too high, and the level of debate too low, for anyone to argue sensibly that her motivation has been justified by events.

Mark Fisher, who died in early 2017, wrote in a famous essay that people interested in political change 'must break out of the "debate" that communicative capitalism ... is endlessly cajoling us to participate in, and remember that we are involved in a class struggle'.[33] It is to the specific nature and behaviour of that communicative capitalism, both in so-called 'legacy media' and in the 'social' online world, that we'll turn for the rest of this book. If we're going to understand those media and see what we can get out of them, we've got to get past idealistic concepts – such as the public sphere – that obstruct our view of the real dynamics at play and of the real struggles in which we need to be engaged.

Choking Off Circulation

Every January, a public relations outfit called Edelman releases the results of a large international online survey on 'trust'. Usually this report can be counted upon to achieve its principal objective: getting Edelman's name into the media. In 2017, however, its conclusions about 'Trust in Crisis' didn't get all that much coverage. Perhaps in the week before Donald Trump's inauguration as president of the US, the survey's conclusion that large numbers of people throughout the world said they didn't trust various elites was classified by editors as 'news' of a similar order of magnitude as 'Bear droppings found in woods'.

Or maybe it wasn't just that the survey was stating the obvious; maybe some of the most striking findings of the survey made editors just a little bit uncomfortable. For example: in Ireland, public trust in the media 'to do what is right' plunged from thirty-nine per cent in the previous year's survey down to twenty-nine per cent, leaving Ireland twenty-seventh of the twenty-eight countries surveyed on this issue. Only people in Turkey were less trusting of the media than people in Ireland. (If it's any consolation to media types, in Ireland trust in the 'credibility' of CEOs fell even faster and further, though the surveyed group showed an unchanged level of trust in government; at thirty-two per cent, government is slightly more trusted than media in Ireland.) In a different report compiled in 2015, it was found that trust in RTÉ had also dropped sharply.[34]

It is difficult to speculate about what such sharp declines reflect or represent. The Edelman survey was conducted in October and November 2016, and may have been affected by widespread and rather cynical discussion about the role of media in the ubiquitous US election. But no other European country showed as big a decline as Ireland, and indeed the US 'trust in media' figure was unchanged from the previous year. Presumably any distrust in media is built upon some not-entirely-conscious combination of, on the one hand, a sense that media outlets don't live up to their stated ambitions to be objective facilitators of a democratic public sphere, and, on the other hand, doubts about the sincerity and feasibility of those ambitions.

This section will probe these grounds for mistrust through the examination of specific cases of apparent media malfeasance in twenty-first-century Ireland: the coverage of the movement against water charges; the coverage of protests against the Iraq invasion and use of Shannon Airport by the US military; and the treatment of the property bubble before and after the financial crisis of 2008. Each of these sections has something to say about the utility and meaning of the public sphere, but the conclusions are not always simple; in the case of Shannon airport, for example, it's clear that media practices may sometimes leave room for counter-hegemonic narratives to emerge in otherwise establishment-friendly newspapers.

In Ireland it may not be too presumptuous to speculate that such public mistrust of the media is personified in one particular media mogul, Denis O'Brien, owner of media-holding company Communicorp and major shareholder in Independent News and Media. In recent years there have been frequent and widely disseminated criticisms (on social media, at least) of O'Brien's dominant role in broadcast and print/web media in Ireland. Perhaps the low trust in Ireland's media flows from this discussion and a sort of popular consciousness about the political economy of mass-media ownership that has resulted.

Discussion of O'Brien's role, however, often tends to exaggerate the direct impact of an owner/shareholder on editorial output, and it also tends to overlook the even more dominant position in Irish media of the state-owned RTÉ. This section won't ignore the much- and appropriately maligned O'Brien, but it will concentrate on trying to grasp the deeper structures of hegemony that determine what happens politically in our media. Seen through this wider lens, the concentration of media ownership may be understood better as a symptom of capitalist hegemony – just another way the system rewards its biggest players – than as one of its primary causes. The ideological role of media under the hegemony of a capitalist state is not reliant on one or other media owner. It fulfils this role, as discussed in Section 1, not (necessarily) by lying, cheating or even overt bias, but by framing issues in a way that effectively limits the terms of any resulting debate.

As media analyst and theorist Stuart Hall wrote in the 1970s, the media 'do some service to maintenance of hegemony, precisely by providing a "relatively independent" and neutral sphere'. This is accomplished, he added, 'not in spite of the rules of objectivity (i.e. by "covert or overt bias") but precisely by holding fast to the communicative forms of objectivity, neutrality, impartiality and balance'.[35] This is not a conspiracy theory, and we should be careful not to exaggerate: some of those positive 'high modernist' journalistic values discussed in Section 1 and recited here by Hall do in fact still result in critical and hard-hitting stories, not just in Hollywood movies and TV shows but in real life. Ultimately, however, the overall effect of media coverage of political controversy can generally be counted upon to legitimate the established systems of business and government, though not necessarily any given player within those systems; and central to that legitimation is precisely the fact that ostensibly critical work is permitted within, and absorbed by, those systems.

Part of the maintenance of legitimacy comes through policing of the limits of debate. Daniel Hallin, whose insights into the changes in journalism over the last three decades were discussed in Section 1, famously divided the press treatment of public issues into three 'spheres'. (Yes, it's spheres again, though in Hallin's diagrams they are really just two-dimensional, concentric circles). At the centre is the sphere of consensus, where the media/political system can see little room for argument – for example, 'Democracy is a good thing.' Beyond that is the sphere of legitimate controversy – you might even call it 'the public sphere' – where the system broadly accepts that there is room for debate among people of good faith – for example, 'How big a budget deficit is acceptable?' (It's arguable that EU rules constitute a neoliberal attempt to move this very question out of the sphere of the debatable.) Then there is the sphere of deviance, which is really the flip side of the sphere of consensus, where we keep ideas that are regarded as out-of-bounds – for example, 'The market is a really terrible way to organise housing' or 'Israel should not be regarded as a legitimate state.'[36] Ideas that are in the sphere of deviance will probably keep you out of the letters page, let alone the editorial boardroom. In reality, of course, the boundaries between spheres can shift, or issues can move. In Ireland, radical critics of both Israel and the housing market have found themselves inching closer to the sphere of legitimate controversy in recent years, and gay marriage has enjoyed a dizzying sprint from deviance to consensus, pausing only briefly for breath, and referendum, in the sphere of legitimate controversy. Nonetheless, the sphere of deviance is generally a tough one from which to escape, and its perimeter is carefully monitored, as shown by the note I got from an *Irish Times* editor in 2003, cited in Section 1, explaining how opposing US military use of Shannon might be acceptable in that newspaper, but the advocacy of civil disobedience in so doing was not. (Arguably, the Shannon question – politics and tactics alike – was moved entirely into the sphere of deviance, where it could be ignored by the media, during the Obama years. There is much more about press treatment of Shannon in 2002 and 2003 below.) The most important issues in Irish public life in recent years – the regime of austerity since the crisis of 2008 and the related popular movement against Irish Water – have given rise to rigorous ideological policing to keep dissent in the sphere of apparent deviance, with studies showing how protesters were framed in the media as belonging to a 'sinister fringe' (a trope that was also very common in coverage of resistance to the Mayo gas pipeline) and opposition to austerity was virtually barred from newspaper opinion columns.[37]

Covering Protest

Within the movement against water charges, this bias did not go unnoticed. An academic survey conducted in late 2014 questioned more than 2,500 people involved in that movement. It found that, asked about the role of the media, forty-five per cent of them said coverage was 'undermining the campaign', and a further forty-one per cent said it was 'unfair'. Respondents' comments were as likely, it seems, to focus on RTÉ as on the privately owned media.[38] This sort of number – nearly nine out of ten respondents selecting a negative conclusion about the role of the media – goes beyond the normal grievances of activists about media bias. These respondents were not, by and large, seasoned activists with long-nurtured critiques of journalism, but new protesters responding to what they saw as distortions of their campaign. Anyone who spent time with fellow Irish users on social-media platforms, especially Facebook, at the height of the anti-water-charges protests will know the anger and disbelief that accompanied media coverage of them. Denis O'Brien was a frequent target – it was widely alleged, though without evidence, that his business interests affected the stories carried by his media outlets – but he was by no means the only one.

Deep class bias coloured the treatment of the anti-water-charges movement, which presented itself not only as a challenge to state policy on water charges that had been consensual across the major parties, but as a challenge based in working-class urban communities that had rarely before erupted with such anger and unity. The combination of fear, condescension and reference to 'outside agitators' reached a pinnacle in November 2014, when a protest in Jobstown – a poor, working-class suburb in south County Dublin – saw senior government minister Joan Burton prevented by the gathered crowd from driving away in police vehicles for more than two hours. The media reacted with hysteria and a depiction of Jobstown residents as out of control and virtually feral – with 'children roaming the streets'. But coverage also focused on the upper-middle-class background of local Dáil deputy Paul Murphy, who was depicted variously as both responsible for the crowd's behaviour and irresponsible for allowing it to be whipped up. It is hard to avoid the conclusion that this media context contributed to the relatively serious charge of 'false imprisonment' being brought against a large number of protesters.[39]

By contrast, the largely middle-class composition of the Irish movement against the war in Iraq in 2002–03, and the relatively remote issues it addressed, gave it a better chance of escaping the sphere of deviance and taking its place in the sphere of legitimate controversy, despite some organisational base in the far left of Irish politics. I was one of the writer-researchers on a large-scale research project into Irish newspaper coverage of that anti-war movement, developed and designed with activists. It demonstrates how protests against the war and the US military's use of Shannon were eventually marginalised as deviant by depicting them as violent and as a potential threat to the economic well-being of the Irish state, but also demonstrates how that marginalisation was delayed by a strategically successful information campaign.[40]

In the fifteen months that preceded the invasion of Iraq, there were more than 100,000 journeys through Shannon Airport by US troops, with almost 35,000 of these in the eleven weeks before the onset of hostilities in March 2003. In late 2002 and January 2003 reports and images of US soldiers passing time in Shannon Airport led to public discussion about how this reflected, and affected, Ireland's traditional status as a 'neutral' state. The American troops stopping at Shannon were on their way to take part in a prospective war that lacked UN approval. The Irish government, when forced to comment, said allowing US-military use of the airport did not constitute participation in any war. US diplomatic cables later released by Wikileaks show that events at the airport and the public debate about its use were a high priority for both the US and Irish governments. The focus of some protesters on Shannon, and the tactics employed there, became a source of tension within the anti-war movement in 2003. (It should be noted here that despite its fraught history, described below, anti-war activity at Shannon has never ceased over the last decade and a half, and Shannonwatch activists continue to keep a close eye on military transport there, informing large numbers of people via social media as they do so.)

Part of the purpose of looking at press coverage of the anti-war movement is to explore the circumstances in which coverage of protest activity may be at least neutral and even sympathetic. Some scholars suggest there is a cycle in which a growing protest campaign may garner positive attention for its grievances before the coverage moves to a focus on conflict and negativity; others suggest protest tactics may be more relevant than goals in triggering negative coverage of a campaign.[41] In the case of Shannon, press coverage might, on the one hand, focus positively on information coming from protesters, and, on the other hand, cast a negative light on protest tactics.

In late 2002 and early 2003 European governments appeared to support a version of the wider anti-invasion position, strengthening the anti-war position in Ireland: the prospect of war was, here, in the sphere of legitimate controversy. In this context, campaigners at Shannon Airport were able to promulgate a 'counter-frame', a way for journalists to frame stories that runs counter to the hegemonic narrative of Irish cooperation with American efforts. But the counter-framing was not entirely successful, partly because of how the press associated violence with protest. As Norman Mailer famously wrote in the 1960s, 'The media are waiting there, like coiled springs, hoping that a few maniacs will cut loose.'

Our research looked at 505 news articles in eleven Irish newspapers, dailies and Sundays, from September 2002 to May 2003 – the entirety of those papers' coverage of the anti-war movement. The time frame captured the escalation of the Iraq crisis in autumn 2002, incorporating the first incidence of 'direct action' against a US military plane at Shannon; the inclusion of stories up to May 2003 took in key events, such as the declaration of 'mission accomplished' by President Bush. This data underlines the importance of the articles studied: these stories that dealt in whole or part with the anti-war movement in Ireland averaged more than ten paragraphs each; forty-four of them appeared on front pages, 111 in the first three pages, 159 in the first five pages, and 245 (nearly half the total) in the first seven pages of their papers. Apart from coverage of a string of Dublin demonstrations in March and April of 2003, the national press largely reserved 'violence' angles, of various kinds, for stories relating to activities at Shannon Airport, where the Irish army was deployed in February 2003 to provide security.

In the autumn of 2002, when anti-war activity was still peripheral and small scale, 'direct action' at Shannon attracted little opprobrium. When activist Eoin Dubsky was arrested at Shannon Airport on 4 September 2002 after marking a US plane with anti-war graffiti, the press largely characterised the incident as a worrying security breach that might suggest Shannon's vulnerability to violent intruders, not as an act of violence in and of itself. There was one clear exception: on 5 September the *Irish Daily Star* published an article with a headline calling Dubsky's action an 'attack'. A 'senior garda [police] source' was quoted as saying, 'If peace activists can get in, I shudder to think who else can try.' Other dailies quoted Garda Inspector Tom Kennedy citing in court an earlier encounter with the defendant at another protest: 'On that occasion he was very uncooperative and is not content to carry out a peaceful protest.' The policeman's implication that graffiti on an airplane constitutes non-peaceful protest attracted no comment and was not widely echoed in the coverage.

Only twenty-five stories about the anti-war campaign scattered across the full range of newspapers returned to the violence theme between the Dubsky incident in September 2002 and a hatchet attack on a US plane by campaigner Mary Kelly at the end of January 2003. The only front-page story was the *Sunday Tribune*'s lead of 12 January 2003, followed up inside the paper, headlined 'Shannon airport target for al Qaeda'. Other newspapers turned to the same specific theme in January as part of their coverage of the growing public knowledge and concern about the use of Shannon by US troops. While these stories do associate the situation at Shannon with the prospect of violence, perhaps contributing to tension around protest there, they do not directly tar the anti-war movement with that association. Indeed, the highlighting of a 'terrorist threat' to Shannon, coming from external Islamists not connected to Irish anti-war protest, could be said to have served the purposes of the anti-war movement; if Shannon were indeed a possible target, then perhaps US troops and equipment should not be facilitated there. There was in this period up to late January no emphasis on violence or the prospect of violence among protesters in the national press.

Even when an emphasis on violence was potentially available, it was little adopted. The national press reacted quietly to the demonstration at Shannon on 12 October 2002 that saw ten people arrested after more than 100 breached a perimeter fence at the airport. In the *Sunday Independent* of 13 October it merited only a short 'news in brief' article on page two, describing an 'unprecedented breach of security by anti-globalisation [*sic*] protesters'. The same day's *Sunday Tribune* had a largely sympathetic interview with Shannon anti-war planespotter Tim Hourigan.

There was an upsurge in coverage of the anti-war movement, focusing on the Shannon issue, in December 2002 and January 2003. After no articles at all in the national press in November 2002, there were fifteen in December and fifty-nine between 1 January and 27 January. This coverage was overwhelmingly along lines that Shannon protesters could be happy with, and it quoted them extensively. Especially in January, these stories were framed predominantly in terms of the information activists on the scene were providing about the scale of US troop activity at the airport, and of the debate they were raising about Irish neutrality in that context. The government's main response was to suggest that nothing unusual was happening at the airport, a tactic that left the authorities highly vulnerable to new information. The Shannon 'peace camp' and 'peace house', sites of protest that rarely hosted more than a few dozen people, saw their frame legitimated during this period across a wide range of newspaper titles. On 7 January the *Irish Independent* ran a large photograph across the top of page nine showing an attractive Shannon protester holding a sign inviting passing motorists to 'bleep for peace'. An accompanying story reported that a group of hillwalkers in Sligo, about 100 miles north of the airport, said they had seen US military planes flying in formation. Its opening phrase may be regarded as emblematic of this period: 'The Department of Foreign Affairs has been unable to explain ...'.

On 9 January 2003 the *Irish Independent*, *Irish Daily Star* and *Evening Herald* all ran big stories about the US troop presence at Shannon, employing the same photo of a handsome young US soldier staring out an airport window. The shot was both poignant and, with its long-lens paparazzi-style flatness, suggestive of a secret that had slipped out. The following day, 10 January, the *Irish Independent* ran a short piece by a political reporter headlined 'Cowen urged to explain role of Shannon in US war move'. Once again, it seemed explanation from Minister for Foreign Affairs Brian Cowen was in short supply. The following weekend, 11 and 12 January, saw the *Irish Examiner*, *Sunday Tribune* and *Ireland on Sunday* devote long, sympathetic articles to the Shannon anti-war campaigners, emphasising the camp's female base and its survival in the face of cold weather. *Ireland on Sunday* on 12 January cited airport workers who provided 'evidence to refute the Government's assurances that the aircraft are unarmed troop carriers'. This question of whether soldiers passing through Shannon were armed, and if so had received permission to carry weapons in Ireland, was a focus of media attention for about a week.

On 13 January 2003 an *Irish Independent* headline, referring to Taoiseach Bertie Ahern, stated: 'Ahern denies Shannon role in build-up to war', though the quotes in the story were more equivocal than the headline suggested. 'I don't think it's correct', he said, apparently in response to claims that the state was knowingly facilitating the movement of weapons through Shannon. The government appeared defensive. The front-page story in the *Irish Examiner* of 14 January 2003 quoted Minister for Foreign Affairs Cowen to the effect that the guns visible on some photographed soldiers were not in fact loaded, and were therefore exempt from notification rules.

The story was largely neglected in the *Irish Times*, until on 18 January its human-interest features writer, Kathy Sheridan, authored an overwhelmingly positive story about the peace camp on the front of the paper's 'Weekend' supplement. Protesters Caoimhe Butterly and Mary Kelly were praised for their previous, and hazardous, Middle East campaigning, and Kelly was paraphrased explaining why they had to camp at Shannon: 'The job, she [Kelly] says, is to monitor the aircraft and to bring this to public attention.' Later in the long piece there was a sympathetic account of the efforts of the Shannon planespotter activist, Tim Hourigan, to debate with Minister for Foreign Affairs Cowen on a TV current-affairs show, and readers were invited to conclude that the minister had evaded the debate because Hourigan would have overwhelmed him with information, based on his direct observations, of US military flights carrying troops and weapons through Shannon. Both Kelly and Hourigan were portrayed as purveyors of information that the government couldn't or wouldn't offer, their role being to 'monitor' activities at Shannon. 'Protest' seemed almost secondary.

The development of the coverage took a decisive turn, however, just a day later. A story in the *Sunday Tribune* on 19 January 2003 by a well-connected political journalist,

Stephen Collins, was effectively a strategic concession of defeat by the government on 'information':

> The Irish government has complained to the US authorities about the failure to provide full information about the number of flights going through Shannon airport carrying military personnel and weapons ... There was concern in government that no notification or late notification had been provided in relation to some of the US flights, but sources say the problem has been rectified.

Analysis of subsequent coverage indicates that this prominent story – which presented the lack of official information about troop and weapons movements through Shannon as a bureaucratic misunderstanding that had now been 'rectified' – marked the abrupt end of protesters' successful information counter-frame. No longer would the anti-war movement earn sympathetic column inches for its 'revelations' about activities at Shannon. The government was no longer denying that things had changed there.

The above-mentioned Mary Kelly, a star of that information counter-frame, was to be central in the framing that followed with considerable intensity: 'violence'. Mary Kelly's hatchet attack on a US Navy plane on the runway at Shannon on 29 January 2003, followed on 3 February by five Catholic Worker activists (the 'Pitstop Ploughshares') damaging the same plane in its repair hangar, were a catalyst for a fundamental change in the dynamic of national-press coverage of the Shannon anti-war movement and its relation to violence, even if the favourable treatment of the 15 February demonstrations in Dublin and around the world tended to obscure and delay that development.

The first press story of Kelly's arrest, on the front page of the *Evening Herald* on 29 January 2003, recycled several paragraphs from a profile that had appeared some days earlier in its sister publication, the *Sunday Independent*. 'Mary Kelly has been described as a globe-trotting professional protester', the un-bylined *Herald* story states, without noting that this description originated with the *Sunday Independent*. The story's third paragraph quotes an unnamed 'investigating officer': 'From what we can make out it was a frenzied attack.' (This suggestion of uncontrolled anger is unique in coverage of anti-war 'violence' in this study.) This story, like one on 30 January in the *Irish Daily Star*, used the word 'Mum' in its headline to refer to Kelly, as if to contrast the ostensibly peaceful, nurturing qualities of motherhood with Kelly's hatchet-wielding exploits. The fact that Kelly was both 'mum' and 'nurse' made her doubly vulnerable to such manufactured irony.

Days later, the Pitstop Ploughshares took their own similar but larger action at Shannon, doing further damage to the same US Navy plane, when they broke into a hangar and hit the aircraft with a pickaxe and hammers.[42] They also built a shrine to the Iraqi victims of bombing and sanctions outside the hangar and daubed slogans including 'Pitstop of Death'. They were eventually arrested without resistance.

This second attack was embarrassing to gardaí and politicians who had said no repetition of the Kelly incident was possible. Some people in the anti-war movement who had been supportive of, or silent about, Kelly expressed opposition to the new Shannon attack. Some were under the impression, based on misleading garda information, that the Catholic Worker group had 'overpowered' a policeman – an allegation that didn't last long enough to feature significantly in print-media coverage of the event, but was prominent for several hours in broadcast coverage.

As with Mary Kelly, because of the early-morning timing of their arrest, the first national-press reporting of the Pitstop Ploughshares incident came in the *Evening Herald*. The newspaper deployed the word 'Catholics' much as it had done 'Mum' for Kelly, with a massive front-page headline 'The Catholics who invaded Shannon', with the subheading 'Second highly embarrassing security breach' (3 February 2003). The article's emphasis on the government's embarrassment and its headline use of the verb 'invade', along with the noun 'raid' in the third paragraph of the article, suggests an upgrading of the press' linguistic arsenal in relation to anti-war activities.

After this second 'invasion', the Irish government and the anti-war movement were now, it seemed, at war in Shannon. The tone was set in an angry broadcast interview with Taoiseach Bertie Ahern, reported in the *Irish Times* and in other newspapers on 4 February. He said: 'Maybe we were a bit over-tolerant of peaceful protesters, when they are not peaceful protesters, carrying hammers, lump hammers and pick-axe handles'. The *Irish Independent* (4 February 2003) headlined on its front page an army–garda 'security ring' at the airport; the same day's *Irish Examiner* lead story called it a 'ring of steel'. The *Irish Times* led with the more restrained 'Cabinet set to approve use of Army to guard US planes' (4 February 2003), while its story on the top of page three described the immediate deployment of armed garda detectives. The impression in this report of a war scene, or at least a Cold War scene, is unmistakable: 'The detectives, armed with Uzi machine guns, were patrolling in icy conditions the immediate vicinity of the old SRS hangar where a US navy cargo aircraft was attacked early yesterday' (4 February 2003). 'Stop, or risk being shot' was the *Irish Daily Star*'s headline response to the same events (4 February 2003). Green Party leader Trevor Sargent was quoted in the *Evening Herald* (4 February 2003) as stating carefully, 'I oppose any law breaking or damage to property which constitutes law breaking', but also saying that he could not state whether these actions constituted law-breaking. In light of the eventual acquittal of the Pitstop Ploughshares in 2006, and the later quashing of Mary Kelly's conviction, Sargent was being far more prescient than any contemporary coverage gave him credit for. He had visited Kelly in jail and knew of the likely, and ultimately successful, legal defence to the charges of criminal damage faced by all the defendants. Virtually no one else was as careful as Sargent; even the *Irish Times* was rash enough to call the accused 'lawbreakers' (editorial, 4 February 2003).

The new atmosphere was sufficient to cause the Shannon peace camp to disband, amid stories of emotional divisions about 'direct action'. Compared to jurisdictions such as the US, where crime coverage is free wheeling, Ireland has a long tradition of criminal courts that don't tolerate press speculation about people who have been charged with a crime. Due to the resulting journalistic caution, Kelly and the Pitstop Ploughshares were rarely directly described with the word 'violent'; the implication tended to arise by contrast with 'peaceful protest', a phrase generally employed as though it were the opposite of their actions. The marginalisation of Kelly and the Pitstop Ploughshares that runs through the media coverage of 4 to 6 February, in particular, was based in part upon statements from elements of the anti-war movement that repudiated them and their acts. This was arguably a case of a protest movement submitting itself to the logic of the media, with its policing of the boundaries of legitimacy. The dynamic created by the direct-action focus on Shannon Airport and the resulting divisions in Irish anti-war activity are peculiar to the Irish movement and media. In contrast to what prevailed in other European countries, Irish media coverage of the anti-war movement had a decidedly negative cast some weeks before war began on 19 March, and not just because of perceived violence, as we'll see shortly.

In the days between 23 February and 3 March 2003, there were about forty separate press stories coded in our study as including 'implication of violence' about the anti-war movement. This outburst is particularly striking, because there were no stories at all in any national newspaper coded in our research as containing any 'implication of violence' on any date from 18 to 22 February, no doubt due to the benign effect of the global 15 February demonstrations, when media around the world bowed to the perceived 'ordinariness' of that day's demonstrations. Shannon was at the centre of the negative, violence-oriented coverage when it resumed, though there wasn't actually a significant protest there – 'direct action' or 'peaceful' – until Saturday 1 March. Every story relating violence to the anti-war movement in late February and early March was concerned in some way with the protests planned and executed at Shannon. Crucial to understanding this construction is the knowledge that two separate demonstrations were scheduled at Shannon for 1 March, one called by the Grassroots Network Against War (GNAW), sympathetic to direct action and calling for a 'mass trespass' at the airport, and another, by the Irish Anti-War Movement (IAWM), assumed to be a 'normal' political march and rally. A further complication was that some groups affiliated to the IAWM disassociated themselves from its protest because of fear that it would be linked with the GNAW action. The distinction between the two protests was lost on reporters and headline writers, who couldn't squeeze this literal plurality into their stories. Headlines reflecting the reality of multiple demonstrations organised by separate groups were rare, and included a presumably tongue-in-cheek one in the *Irish Times* on the day of the protest: 'Irish peace movements deny split' (1 March 2003).

Both the refusal to acknowledge two demonstrations and the excitement about security arrangements are typified by a story in the *Irish Examiner* on 1 March: 'Soldiers added razor wire to Shannon Airport's perimeter fences last night as the army and gardaí braced for trouble at today's anti-war protest.' Such stories often featured successive quotes from groups characterising their own demonstrations as 'peaceful' as a means of contrasting them with others – and on this point journalists cannot be blamed, since groups were spinning against each other.

The avowedly symbolic action proposed by GNAW, to reach and tear down the perimeter fence, and by tearing it down to demonstrate the insecurity of the airport, was understandably turned by both the press and rival campaigners into 'the prospect of violence', but without any analysis of how that violence was most likely to come about, that is, through the 'riot tactics' of the police who were 'braced for trouble'. (The unlikelihood of the protesters reaching and breaching the fence, given the pre-publicity and police presence, was never mentioned.) The riot squad was an object of journalistic interest, featuring in near-identical *Irish Daily Star* headlines on 26 February ('Riot cops at Shannon') and 27 February ('Riot cops to head for Shannon'), and the more excitable

Irish Independent, 'Riot squad to lead charge on airport protesters' (28 February 2003). An *Irish Independent* headline (27 February) cited a 'threat of violence'.

Reports after the fact were of necessity rather anti-climactic. 'Gardai hold off rampage at Shannon' was the dramatic headline in the *Sunday Independent* (2 March 2003) over a report that called the event 'good natured'. So we can see that while violence framing did come to dominate press coverage of anti-war activities at Shannon, this only occurred after late January 2003. The attachment of an implication of violence to aspects of anti-war activity, though rarely entirely absent, was prevalent in the print media for about five weeks, from the time of campaigner Mary Kelly's 'disarmament' with a small axe of a US Navy aircraft at the airport on 29 January until the coverage of protest events of 1 March, when competing factions of the anti-war movement converged on the airport. This month-long period of violence framing coincided with the height of the anti-war movement's popularity and visibility; one may only speculate about its possible contribution to the movement's rapid dissipation.

However, these research findings are by no means all bad news. There was, at the turn of 2002–03, a brief period of frequent and positive coverage of the anti-war movement at Shannon, peaking in mid-January 2003. The research suggests this was not simply a phase in a cycle, but that the movement's successful dissemination in the press of a counter-frame was contingent on poor information from official sources, and the capacity of protesters present at and near the airport to provide data of their own. It became clear, given the availability of visual evidence largely supplied by activists, that the Irish government could not sustain assertions that there was nothing new or different about the US-military's use of Shannon in this period. However, once Irish officials admitted that Shannon was involved in transporting large numbers of troops and munitions, claiming they had been kept in the dark themselves by their the US counterparts, sympathetic exposure of the anti-war movement's information counter-frame vanished completely, soon to give way to implications of violence, and to concerns about the possible 'economic consequences' of opposing the war against Iraq.

When the anti-war movement in Ireland could be portrayed as the medium for a specific version of liberal moral unease, it was often fêted in the press. When anti-war protesters could be constructed as representing a challenge to the essential political economy of the state, it was a different story. The press rarely took the lead in making such arguments, but when the government of the day, and especially the Tánaiste (deputy prime minister) Mary Harney, began to attack the movement for putting the economy in danger, the assertions were reported and repeated uncritically.

In February and March of 2003, in contrast to the way Shannon activists had earlier been allowed to share their impressions of activity at the 'warport', the familiar reliance of journalists on official sources and interpretations ensured that the national press tended to cast the anti-war movement as a danger to both the regional and national economies. Anti-war activists were rarely quoted contesting this (largely nonsensical) narrative of risk. This demonstrates one notable aspect of media behaviour, whether or not we understand it in terms of the ideal of the public sphere: public-affairs media are by their nature concerned with policing the limits of dissent, with defining what kind of ideas are allowed in 'the sphere' and what needs to be kept out. This need not be regarded conspiratorially, but rather, from the viewpoint of journalists, as a matter of keeping matters neat, respectable and responsible. In the period leading up to 15 February, the media conceded that the impending invasion and Shannon's role in it were matters of legitimate public controversy, within the sphere. However, beginning in late February 2003, political elites successfully constructed the anti-war movement as being somehow outside the sphere of legitimate debate, because it might put the consensually beloved 'economy' at risk. Protesters, somewhat inadvertently, threatened to draw greater attention to Ireland's deepening economic dependence on foreign capital, a dependence that would explode in Irish faces when a global financial crisis wrecked the economy in 2008.

'We all partied'

It was absurd to imagine that the US multinationals making enormous profits in Ireland cared particularly about whether the US military used Shannon Airport. Still, the press's readiness to amplify the voices that whined about dangerous 'economic consequences' of anti-war activity here suggest a deeper loyalty, not merely to the US but to the myths of unfettered capitalism that were intertwined with newspapers' own profits: Tigerish growth in general, and the property bubble in particular, were good for business.

Newspapers, it must be understood, were not simply beneficiaries of the late-Celtic Tiger property bubble. As a number of property-industry insiders have assured me, it could not have happened without them. Until the early twenty-first century, at any rate, 'the property market' was, in effect, synonymous with the property pages of newspapers, and particularly of mid-market and upmarket newspapers such as the *Irish Independent* and *Irish Times*. Those papers did not simply report the market and benefit from the growth of the market; they *were* the market, a market that could not have bubbled without newspapers blowing.[43]

More broadly, both print and broadcast media in Ireland played an immeasurable but certainly significant role in the inflation of the property bubble and the legitimation of risky behaviour by the financial-services sector, involving both Irish and international banks, in the lead-up to the crisis of 2007–08, and did so partly by ignoring or marginalising scepticism about these phenomena. This socially destructive role should be understood not as a 'failing' of Irish newspapers but as a feature, one that flows predictably from the commercial-media's structural relationship with the corporate forces that benefited from the bubble. While this relationship is of very long standing and continues, to some extent, to this day, there were certain aspects of the development of newspapers in the 1990s and early 2000s – particularly acute in Ireland, but also experienced elsewhere in the world – that made them especially vulnerable to domination by those corporate forces, and weakened the capacity of journalists to play the critical, adversarial, investigative role that most of them undoubtedly value, at least in theory.

As discussed already, these principles, often brought together with claims of objectivity and impartiality under the rubric of 'professionalism', are widely understood to be increasingly at risk all over the world, with particular features of the media landscape endangering them. As Hallin has written: 'For the most part I don't think journalistic professionalism is breaking down from the inside, by journalists becoming less committed to it; instead I think professionalism is being squeezed into increasingly smaller niches within the media field.'[44] In Irish newspapers we can literally see that 'squeeze' occur over the period between about 1990 and 2007, as the physical construction of newspapers changed. These changes coform closely to, and are the most dramatic visible manifestations of, the commercialisation of the media by advertising and PR that, in Habermas' own original formulation, destroyed the public sphere in the twentieth century. In the late twentieth century here in Ireland, there was an inscription of an unquestioning and *explicit* pro-business ideology and practice onto increasingly large, advertising-heavy portions of newspapers, with ever-growing business/finance, property and lifestyle sections dedicated to the advertising of, respectively, recruitment, real-estate and consumer goods and services. Even the most scrupulous of newspaper editors came to see those sections as a realm of, at best, what you might call 'professionalism lite', where soft treatment of the rich and powerful and celebrated was to be expected. Even if you worked in the niches where full-blown professionalism still held sway (if you were responsible for filling news pages and providing political coverage, for example), it was hard to miss the message embedded in that big, colourful product about your employer's relationship to financial institutions, property interests and other corporate bodies. Those supplements were, after all, paying the bills. When Irish Times Ltd infamously paid €50 million for myhome.ie in 2006, it appeared to confirm its dedication to what increasingly looked like its core business: advertising property sales. This has obvious consequences, of course, for the newspaper's capacity to deal impartially with subjects such as the desirability of property ownership over other forms of tenure, or the related question of the 'soft landing', that is, the idea that when the market calmed down, it would do so gently rather than fall precipitously.

A group of Irish financial journalists, speaking on condition of anonymity to a team of academic researchers that published their findings in 2010, discussed this issue. One of them said: 'Much of the mainstream media seems to me to be very conflicted because of their reliance on real-estate and recruitment advertising. That doesn't mean reporters consciously avoid writing bad news stories, but it's hard to run against the tide when everyone is getting rich.' Another stated that journalists 'were leaned on by their organisations not to talk down the banks [and the] property market because those organisations have a heavy reliance on property advertising.'[45]

In 2006 I interviewed dozens of journalists for an article in the *Dubliner* magazine about the political direction of the *Irish Times*. One of them, retired from the paper, said: 'In the mid-1980s ... we had a series investigating the truth behind buying and selling property. Can you imagine that now?' Even in the 1980s, he recalled, 'The commercial side of the paper [that is, those who sold advertising] were in complaining like nobody's business' about the series, but editor Douglas Gageby 'stood up to them'.

The idea that certain, then-small parts of Irish newspapers were professionally compromised territory, however, was already in the air as early as the 1980s. A former business editor from Independent Newspapers recalled a lunch from that period where journalists and brokers gathered to mark the appointment of a new president of the Irish Stock Exchange:

The lunch went well and all the proprieties were observed, until, during the port, the topic of mutual dependence came up in the conversation. 'What do you mean, mutual?' a rubicund and slightly tipsy broker ventured. 'The business pages are ours. We own them.' ... Trudging back to the office ... I admit an icy feeling was coursing through my veins. Maybe, the chap with the English public school accent was right. He was implying that we were lazy, dependent and largely uncritical. More chillingly still, maybe our employers (who shared the same gentlemen's clubs with the brokers) were happy with such an arrangement.[46]

By the time of the Celtic Tiger, this compromised turf of business and financial journalism had expanded many times over, both in the volume of pages produced and in the number of journalists employed. In that important and revealing research cited earlier, the authors summarise the views of several of the Irish financial journalists they interviewed:

According to Journalist F, because of the need for regular contact with financial sources, 'some journalists are reluctant to be critical of companies because they fear they will not get information or access in the future'. Journalist E ... believed that some journalists had become 'far too close to their sources': They viewed them as friends and allies and essentially became advocates for them. Their approach was justified editorially because many developers and bankers limited access to such an extent that it became seen to be better to write soft stories about them than to lose access.

Extremely soft stories would be run to gain access too ... Journalist B criticised daily financial journalism for being 'almost entirely press release and stock exchange disclosure based' ... Journalist F noted, it was 'well known that some PR companies try to bully journalists by cutting off access or excluding journalists from briefings'.[47]

This sort of ambivalence, to put it kindly, about telling good, tough stories while maintaining source relationships is not unique to financial and property journalism. However, as the role and prominence of those sorts of journalism increased exponentially in the 1990s and early 2000s, their particular compromises of 'professionalism' played a proportionately much bigger role in newspaper coverage of these important areas of the economy and society. Their growth was not inevitable, nor unique to Ireland. It was part of an international development in the newspaper industry that sought to diversify papers' content and appearance to make them more attractive to advertisers and (to a lesser extent) readers. In the US in the late 1980s and early 1990s, this came to be known as 'total newspapering', with a de-emphasis on 'news' and – here's the 'total' part – an effort to break down traditional barriers between editorial and commercial considerations.[48] Also known as 'market-led journalism', it was already worrying practitioners cited in British research in the 1990s: 'Among journalists there are fears that the delicate balance between the self-interest of capitalist media owners and the "public interest" motives of journalism has been upset ... Some journalists have come to believe that the news is being stolen from them.'[49] This market orientation does not express itself merely in the growth of financial and property journalism, but in the explosion of entertainment, lifestyle and consumer-oriented sections and stories. As one scholar summarises it:

> When market orientation is high, journalism gives emphasis to what the audiences want to know at the expense of what they should know ... Audiences are not addressed in their role as citizens concerned with the social and political issues of the day but in their role as clients and consumers ... A journalistic orientation to the logic of the marketplace crystallizes in a journalistic culture that provides help, advice, guidance, and information about the management of self and everyday life ... The materialization of infotainment news and lifestyle journalism exemplifies this trend toward a blending of information with advice and guidance as well as with entertainment and relaxation.[50]

These developments in newspapers did not, of course, happen by accident or in isolation. As David Harvey has explained: 'Neoliberalization required both politically and economically the construction of a neoliberal market-based populist culture of differentiated consumerism and individual libertarianism.'[51]

It is important to note that we shouldn't blame most journalists individually or collectively for this situation, and they have not been its obvious beneficiaries. Even in Ireland, where the booming economy helped news paper circulation and profitability to remain healthy past the year 2000, a journalistic culture of increased workloads, casualisation, rapidly changing technological expectations and declining real rates of pay was in place throughout the industry even before the wider bust of 2007–08. When I interviewed newspaper journalists in 2006, many of them told me that their capacity to engage in critical scrutiny of government and business was overwhelmed by the day-to-day pressures of filling ever-more space in print and online; the old newsroom where reporters worked within fields of specialisation and might labour for days and weeks on stories before publishing anything had already changed beyond recognition. The job of careful consideration and analysis of events was largely left to a small coterie of editors and senior political writers, who generally rose to those posts through a combination of caution and conservatism. As research elsewhere has also suggested, journalists who continued to feel that they should be doing hard-hitting, critical scrutiny of powerful institutions felt disempowered from doing so. These conditions have, if anything, deteriorated further in the intervening years of collapsing circulation and desperate digitisation; as one leading scholar has put it, the prevalent online-media practice is 'encouraging journalists to rely more on a restricted pool of tried-and-tested news sources as a way of generating increased output. And in general, it is giving rise to a more officebound, routine, and scissors-and-paste form of journalism.'[52] This generalisation, published eight years ago, puts it mildly, as such 'churnalism' has become more and more the norm in legacy- and new-media companies alike.

Such conditions also provide the context for the increasing power of the public-relations industry. As noted above, the capacity of PR officers to give and withhold the information that hard-pressed journalists require in order to do their work gives them an inevitable influence over content, to the benefit of their state and corporate clients. An even more insidious form of PR influence comes in the form of 'flak', the negative attention and pressure that journalists come under when they attempt to report on sensitive stories. In theory, flak can come from any side of a story; in practice, most of it comes from the sides that can afford to generate it at a volume and with a social standing that catches the ear of editors. For most journalists with a busy job to do, this sort of thing becomes a good reason to ignore a story, or at least avoid its more 'controversial' elements.

Of course the most fearsome, ear-catching flak of all is the stuff an owner or major shareholder might fire off, flak that is to be avoided at all costs if you want to keep your job or, more likely these days, your irregular casualised work. By their nature, the corpses that litter a newsroom because of an owner's power are almost impossible to identify. Media critics, indeed, get rather excited when we do get an unimpeachably solid story of a journalist apparently victimised for offending an owner; in Ireland that means the story of Sam Smyth, a leading journalist who lost positions in both the *Irish Independent* and Today FM, and who had drawn attention to public controversies involving Denis O'Brien, who owned the radio station and has a substantial interest in the newspaper.[53] But the damage done by a powerful owner with widespread business interests consists mainly of stories that never get approached, let alone written. When that owner is Denis O'Brien, who is also inclined to sue journalists and publications that offend him, the silencing of critics and investigators extends far beyond the newsrooms where he might wield direct influence. Fear of litigation is almost as effective a silencer as fear of the boss. Getting sued is costly and time-consuming, even when you're sure you're legally in the right. Publications routinely maintain informal lists of people who are more or less unmentionable, their names virtually unpublishable, for this very reason. Needless to say, these people are almost uniformly rich and powerful.

Ireland is a small country with an especially big media-ownership problem and successive governments that don't seem to mind. O'Brien was permitted to increase his power over media companies shortly before the long-delayed 2014 Competition Act put a few potential restrictions on such acquisitions; the relevant minister, Alex White, noted with apparent regret that the law couldn't be applied retrospectively. Europe-wide research on media policy and pluralism found Ireland to be at particularly high risk in relation to the concentration of media ownership.[54]

However, as the discussion above of the media politics of protest and of property bubbles has suggested, ownership of media cannot tell the whole story about the media: the *Irish Times* is owned by a trust, but has not been immune to the commercial pressures discussed here. Indeed, the *Irish Times* is probably the most deeply implicated of all media in Ireland's financial crisis; there was a congruence of interests between a media organisation that provided the principal marketplace for high-end property speculation and the developers and financiers who were cashing in handsomely on a speculative bubble. While much of the professional practice of journalism is conducted with an acute and value-laden awareness of 'how it should be done' – producing hard-hitting stories that afflict the powerful – nonetheless a plethora of other influences determines the shape and content of the journalistic product, leading to Celtic Tiger biases in favour of, for example, 'talking up' the economy, the market, home ownership and the soft landing. This congruence of interests might have been 'stronger', that is to say more consistently and widely influential, than any conflict of interest between the newspaper's market position and the professional values of its journalists.

What, then, about our public-service broadcaster? RTÉ is owned by the people of Ireland, but it has not been immune to blowing bubbles. Its role in broadcasting 'property porn' in the boom years, in television programmes that often had sponsorship from the financial and insurance industries that were riding the Tiger, certainly bears scrutiny. RTÉ's dual-funding model, whereby just over half its budget comes from the licence-payers of Ireland, with the balance being mostly advertising revenue, is reflected in its often frankly commercial priorities. And as noted above, RTÉ tends to attract special opprobrium from activists for its more-than-occasional resemblance to an official state broadcaster; its news correspondents almost visibly adhere to the politicians and other officials whom they cover, and there is a narrow range of opinion, converging in the centre-right, on its radio and TV discussion programmes. More than once I've been approached by campaigners who wanted my support for an effort to abolish the licence fee and, with it, RTÉ itself. I've never signed up. In my view, to paraphrase Winston Churchill's famous line about democracy, RTÉ is the worst Irish broadcaster, except for all the others.

Despite its cuts and redundancies in recent years, it still has the most journalists, though like other outlets it has engaged in rampant casualisation of their employment. Its investigations unit, for all the arguments you can have about its priorities, dwarfs anything similar in the state, and its public funding means it has the most 'sustainable business model' – to use that dreadful phrase – of any media outlet here. A much-crippled but even better public-service broadcaster, the BBC, provides most of the best news and current affairs that Northern Ireland gets (as well as a good chunk of the worst).

You don't have to believe in deliberative democracy or a perfect Habermasian public sphere to understand that people should have access to reasonably accurate information about public affairs, and you don't have to look much further than your nearest commercial-media outlet – which is either producing utter garbage, is on its last legs financially, or, most likely, both – to see that a publicly funded information system is the best way to ensure there is some chance of people having such access.

There remain severe problems, not least the question of how we can globalise a more democratic and public-ly controlled information order, beyond the occasional but limited excellence of some national public media. But when the Rupert Murdochs and TV3s of the world attack public service broadcasting, complaining it enjoys an unfair advantage in the marketplace, we need to step in and say: you're damn right it does, because it belongs to all of us. By all means let's fight to improve the service; let's argue about funding schemes that are more progres-sive than the flat tax that is the licence fee in both Irish jurisdictions; let's campaign to ensure that RTÉ and the BBC are truly public, with democratic input and mean-ingful consultation rather than being oriented toward more commercialisation and corporate partnership;[55] but let's not allow any more lasting damage to be done to these precious public assets.

It's not just a gut feeling or state-sector bias or a knee that invariably jerks leftward that leads me to this position. Again and again, throughout the world, research has told us that public service media remain different from and (dare we say) better than their private-sector counterparts. Sure, commercial broadcasters pour out more and more news, broadcast and online, but a review of the global literature conducted recently concludes that 'public service media remain distinctly different from market-driven news, and that they clearly are more effective in engendering informed citizenship'.[56]

If that rather paternalistic, publicly spherical language of 'engendering informed citizenship' makes you a little suspicious, a little twitchy, that's good. I could not have written those words myself without the inverted commas around them. We know we often have little reason to trust the information that comes from our public-service media, not least because they are part of a media ecosystem that transcends the 'public–private' divide; information and misinformation circulate with equal facility across that boundary, as countless studies have also shown. After all, it was an RTÉ reporter who first said – wrongly and prejudicially – that the Pitstop Ploughshares might face more serious charges for 'overpowering a garda' at Shannon Airport. It was another, more recently, who appeared to have been caught up in the efforts to spin against a police whistleblower.[57]

It's complicated. You don't have to believe that a capitalist state could possibly support a genuinely useful and truly fair media outlet to believe that it might support a better one than the market does. You can understand the hegemonic role of state media while understanding that hegemony invariably leaves gaps.

You can strategically employ a defence of the idea of public-service media as part of a wider defence of the public sector. In other words, critical support for public-service media is not the same as faith in the idea of the public sphere. What is nearly impossible to do is imagine a reliable information regime without some element of public support. The alternatives, be they market-based or philanthropic, are simply not up to the task.[58]

We may think about Utopias later in this book. Until then, we have to defend some ideas and structures that we won't find when we achieve the best of all possible worlds. We can reach across the hegemonic boundary and support the public-service broadcaster. We can even do so while employing some of the language of journalistic high modernism. The ultimate implausibility of an impartial, critical, watch-dogged fourth estate incorporating, as a major component, state-supported media is less important than the fact that the image holds some cultural purchase and can therefore be useful in building a popular struggle for something better.

But we should defend those ideas and build that struggle with eyes wide open and trained upon the gap between image and reality. The same television network that presented the idealised media world of *Lou Grant* four decades ago delivered a very different message, and showed its true colours, more recently. Early in 2016 the president of CBS, Leslie Moonves, gazed upon the circus that Donald Trump was making of the US presidential election, looked at the advertising revenue, and declared to an audience of tech-finance business people: 'Man, who would have expected the ride we're all having right now? ... The money's rolling in and this is fun.' He continued: 'Sorry. It's a terrible thing to say. But, bring it on, Donald. Keep going ... It may not be good for America, but it's damn good for CBS.'[59]

Likes, Shares
and Leaves

For centuries, the business model of most commercial media has been the very one that Leslie Moonves celebrated so movingly in his 'bring it on, Donald' speech, quoted at the end of Section 2. Getting audiences to pay for access to content is all well and good, but it's not always necessary; the real money gets made when you get advertisers to pay for access to audiences. A newspaper such as the *Irish Times*, with a circulation that surpassed 100,000 copies per day for only a few years around the turn of the millennium, couldn't survive financially, and couldn't charge the highest advertising rates in the market, if it didn't have such a tasty, prosperous readership to offer to companies. The falls in circulation it has suffered (along with other newspapers), sharp though they've been, would have been less damaging if they had not been accompanied by more precipitous declines in advertising revenue. Irish companies, especially during the boom years, were more lavish than their counterparts in most other countries when it came to splashing cash in newspapers. These days their love is spread much more thinly across multiple platforms.

In Section 2 we discussed some consequences for the newspaper press of that relationship and the changes in it. The reason I return to it here is that, for all the talk of a radical rupture in the media business thanks to the Internet, and for all the problems of new distribution models that have arisen, the reliance on corporate advertising represents continuity more than change in the fundamental political economy of media, old and new. The peculiar qualities of our networked information environment, I argue in this section, may tend to obscure this most fundamental of continuities: that our media are vehicles for commercial messaging; the main difference is that we are now often the messengers as well as the messaged.

There are of course many media and many messages worth celebrating in this brave old and new world, but we need to push back against a rhetoric that confuses the pleasures (and pressures) of apparently infinite pluralism with visions of real communicative freedom and political power. We can no longer imagine online engagement as a substitute for 'real world' politics, given how thoroughly the real and online worlds are intertwined – and not only in Donald Trump's Twitter feed – but we can look closely at the 'real' content of virtual politics amid the allegedly special features of the online world such as 'fake news'.

For centuries, advertising has been hyped as the midwife of press freedom, removing journalism from the sponsorship of governments and factions. However, nearly 200 years ago the radical journalist William Cobbett was buying none of that talk:

> I perceive that you want very much to be enlightened on the state of our press, which you appear to regard as being free, and which, as I am going to prove to you, is the most enslaved and the vilest thing that has ever been heard of in the world under the name of press. I say, that I am going to prove this; and proof consists of undeniable facts, and not of vague assertions.
>
> Advertising is the great source of revenue with our journals, except in very few cases, such as mine, for instance, who have no advertisements. Hence, these journals are an affair of trade and not of literature; the proprietors think of the money that is to be got by them; they hire men to write them; and these men are ordered to write in a way to please the classes who can give most advertisements. The Government itself pays large sums in advertisements, many hundreds a year, to some journals. The aristocracy, the clergy, the magistrates (who are generally clergy too) in the several counties; the merchants, the manufacturers, the great shopkeepers; all these command the press, because without their advertisements it cannot be carried on with profit.[60]

Cobbett himself scarcely represented the only resistance to the commercial command of capital and nobility in the 1830s; indeed, an especially spirited, radical, working-class press emerged in Britain in the years just after he wrote these words. Nonetheless, resistance was to prove futile. The great historian of the British press, James Curran, sums up the story of the sector in the years after Cobbett: 'Market forces succeeded where legal repression had failed in conscripting the press to the social order in mid-Victorian Britain.'[61]

Any discussion of contemporary media that does not start with the command of capital and the continuing dominance of market forces, through advertising and beyond advertising, is one that is fairly certain to miss the point by a wide margin. While many newspapers are failing because they can't sustain print and online publication on the money that comes in from advertising (plus sales and subscriptions), most of the new-media outlets and platforms that have appeared over the last two decades are funded mainly through some form of advertising and sponsorship. One particularly insidious form of advertising, which was present but mostly peripheral in much of the newspaper press of the twentieth century, is 'embedded' or 'native' advertising: material that looks just like normal 'content' (journalism) but is in fact being paid for by a sponsor. In the old days we used to call it 'advertorial'. There is traditionally some small print to give the reader a clue about what's going on: 'advertising feature' or 'sponsored content', for example. The story and its relation to the advertiser might take various forms, from an uncritical profile of a company to something a bit more sideways. To cite three recent and real examples, it might be a listicle about why we love chocolate, sponsored by Cadbury's; or advice for young people trying to save money, sponsored by KBC Bank; or reports on efforts to stem gang violence in Honduras, sponsored by coffee company Kenco.

One interesting consequence of the rise of native advertising has been the parallel rise of Donald Trump. Trump owed his A-list, ubiquitous, post-millennial celebrity – as opposed to mere rich-guy notoriety – to a television format, *The Apprentice*, that is especially profitable because of the 'brand integration' opportunities it provides. The would-be business people on the reality TV show perform tasks involving real-life companies, and each episode has a single conspicuous and high-paying corporate sponsor. Without such a revenue stream, there would have been no *Apprentice*; without *The Apprentice*, it is safe to say, there would have been no President Trump. (The Donald's political ascent through the realm of anti-Obama conspiracy theory is, of course, another dimension of his absurdly terrible success story.) The extent to which 'reality' is altered on such shows for the sake of sponsors is clear. Trump, as executive producer, also benefited from the actions of a production team whose first priority was to make him look good. People who have never watched Trump's *Apprentice* might assume he's just a bully who likes to say 'You're fired.' In fact, the show portrayed him as a good guy who offered friendly mentoring and made rational decisions about the show's winners and losers. The supervising editor on the first six seasons of the show, Jonathan Braun, explains:

> Our first priority on every episode ... was to reverse-engineer the show to make it look like his judgment had some basis in reality. Sometimes it would be very hard to do, because the person he chose did nothing. We had to figure out how to edit the show to make it work, to show the people he chose to fire as looking bad – even if they had done a great job.[62]

In other words, *The Apprentice* presented something very different from reality, and Donald Trump rose to celebrity and power amidst the ethical and legal free-for-all that governs media purporting to depict events and issues from the real world. It is hard to imagine that a US TV network such as NBC, which shows the programme, would have accepted such propagandistic distortions in a 'documentary' format thirty or forty years ago. Such is the corporate capture of broadcasting's value system that such mediated lying is taken for granted in the twenty-first century. Now, as a consequence, NBC and the other networks have to report on a president whose decision-making cannot be reverse engineered at the end of the week to look as though it were rational (or can it?). But hey, Trump is good for NBC as well as CBS.

Such corporatised 'reality' is now ubiquitous. It's hard to believe that even a few years ago there was controversy about celebrities such as Kim Kardashian – some of whom were themselves 'manufactured' in the fake world of 'reality' – getting paid to tweet on behalf of corporate sponsors. Today, there are people whose celebrity essentially consists of the fact that they tweet (and Snapchat and Instagram) on behalf of corporate sponsors. Known as 'social influencers', they monetise their social media presence by attracting payment for some of their posts. Sometimes you can click through a link in the post and buy products, with a cut of the payment going to the poster.[63] As Jay! (*sic*) Tomlinson of the *Best of the Left* podcast regularly describes the shopping experience via the Amazon link on his website, 'You don't pay any extra, and 7 to 8 per cent of your order in soulless, corporate blood money goes to help the production of this show.'

In our cynical societies, this sort of transparency makes the whole arrangement look almost innocent. However, in late 2016 the concept of 'social-media influencing' took a new and altogether more sinister turn. Suddenly, it seemed that 60 million US voters had been influenced by fake news generated in, among other places, Macedonian click-farms, to elect an orange alt-right narcissist as their president.[64] Never mind that the previous Republican Party candidate for president, Mitt Romney in 2012, had also won about 60 million votes without help from Macedonia, and with an unquestionably stronger opponent (plus, of course, less effective geographic distribution of his votes). No, as with journalism before, there was widespread liberal willingness to ignore deeper systemic issues and decide that when it came to the American political system, the Internet broke it. Someone, probably working for Vladimir Putin, had mastered search-engine optimisation, the Facebook algorithm and online human psychology to such perfection that voters could be clickbaited all the way into fascism.

With its alarming and alarmist techno-dystopianism, like a mind-control tale from bad science fiction, and an explanatory power that bordered on the conspiratorial (and often crossed the border), the fake-news thesis had everything going for it except truth. A study published on the website of the prestigious *Columbia Journalism Review* in January 2017, using what was arguably a too-broad definition of 'fake news', nonetheless found that 'the fake news audience is tiny compared to the real news audience – about 10 times smaller on average'. It also found that 'the real news audience spiked' in the run-up to and around the 2016 presidential election, while fake news didn't see any election-season increase in readership. Perhaps most tellingly, the study 'found that the fake news audience does not exist in a filter bubble. Visitors to fake news sites visited real news sites just as often as visitors to real news sites visited other real news sites.'[65] Another study, at Stanford University, found that fake news had a low impact and that the three 'most believed' fake stories of the election season favoured Hillary Clinton rather than Trump.[66] About the only thing that was true in the familiar narrative of the fake-news panic was that – you guessed it – Facebook was disproportionately responsible for sending people to it.

Inevitably, the excitement and credulity of the fake-news panic led reputable publications to report what can only be described as fake news. The most notorious, and among the most widely shared, was an effort by the *Washington Post* to smear a wide range of news and comment websites as either 'useful idiots' or active arms of Russian fake-news propaganda.[67] Alongside the smearing of almost anything outside the mainstream, the legacy-news outlets have used 'fake news' as a marketing campaign, a way of positioning themselves as the opposite of fake: 'Real journalism. Like nowhere else', the subscription link at nytimes.com promises. (This from the newspaper that infamously and falsely reported, in the lead-up to the invasion of Iraq, that Saddam Hussein had weapons of mass destruction.) In the midst of the hype, many mainstream journalists got to vent their dislike of Julian Assange and Wikileaks, which, despite never having published anything inaccurate or untrue, was accused of doctoring emails and tarred with the 'Russian propaganda for Trump' brush.

There's a problem with all this that goes well beyond the opportunism of certain journalists and news outlets who want to cast themselves as the white knights ready to rescue the public sphere from white-haired hackers, evil algorithmic geniuses and Putin's dastardly clutches. It is this: all the panic about the sinister influencers, propagandists and fake-newsers who are profiting from our attachment to Facebook rather distracts attention from the extent to which Facebook itself profits from our attachment to Facebook. After all, the sponsored beauty vloggers and Macedonian click-farmers are just Internet entrepreneurs, and highly precarious ones in the 'gig economy' at that, vulnerable to shifts in taste and algorithm that could carry them away from profitable eyeballs in an instant. Facebook, on the other hand, owns the platform and everything we post on it, a portfolio that earned the company $4.7 *billion* in profits in the third quarter of 2017 *alone* (emphasis added out of sheer amazement). It has 1.37 billion daily users, more than ninety per cent of whom use the platform on mobile devices. In the first quarter of 2016, eighty-five per cent of the digital advertising spend in the US went to Facebook and Google.[68]

With the possible exception of the Chinese and US governments, no entities in human history have ever held so much information about so many people as Facebook and Google do. The uses of data on this scale, to market to and manipulate individuals and groups, have only begun to be understood. Predictably enough, and with more justification than the hyperventilation over fake news, 'big data' has been at the centre of nightmarish stories about its role in electing Donald Trump. With information gathered and bought from all over the Internet, Cambridge Analytica (a British-founded company of which Trump's former advisor Steve Bannon is a director) did granular-level electoral targeting for Trump based on psychological profiles calculated from voters' online behaviours:

On the day of the third presidential debate between Trump and Clinton, Trump's team tested 175,000 different ad variations for his arguments, in order to find the right versions, above all via Facebook. The messages differed for the most part only in microscopic details, in order to target the recipients in the optimal psychological way: different headings, colors, captions, with a photo or video.[69]

Trump, as we learn from a particularly dark and dystopian account of his data-driven campaign first published in Swiss magazine Das, 'invested far more in digital than TV campaigning compared to Hillary Clinton'. The chief executive of Cambridge Analytica, Alexander Nix, is quoted in the article telling a US conference audience that traditional blanket advertising is dead; 'My children will certainly never, ever understand this concept of mass communication.'[70] This vision – of every message individually targeted, of every messenger being able to get inside your head thanks to thousands of data points you've left behind online, and of the death and erasure of communications aimed at mass audiences – is surely the strangest and scariest that the contemporary media system has thrown up. It is a picture in which the Internet looks like one giant experiment, and we're the lab rats – electrodes plunged into us, via our phones, to extract our privacy, our loyalty, our principles and our money.

It is hard to believe in this context that just a few years ago the cutting-edge scholarly caution was against an 'overcelebratory approach towards new media' in an environment where the 'dispersed, globalised and distributed nature of contemporary audience activity is such that traditional research methods struggle to capture experiences and forms of practice that are, in themselves, fluid and constantly changing'.[71] Even where the Internet was understood as a series of transactions, neologisms such as 'prosumption' (a combination of production and consumption, the sort of thing we do when we review an item on Amazon or upload as well as view YouTube videos) signalled what were seen as interesting shifts in agency and even power. Everywhere you looked, in popular culture and in media studies, too, the Internet's participatory, democratic potential was being highlighted. Indeed, so many commentators believed this potential was already being fulfilled in the likes of Iran's Green Revolution that Eugeny Morozov had to write a celebrated demolition of 'cyber-utopianism and Internet-centrism'. The quotes Morozov assembles in the opening section of 2011's *The Net Delusion* seem to come from another world, where instead of fretting about, or nervously mocking, Donald Trump's tweets, the opinion columns of the world's newspapers were celebrating 'Twitter-powered revolutions'; as Morozov wrote: 'Technology, with its unique ability to fuel consumerist zeal – itself seen as a threat to any authoritarian regime – as well as its prowess to awaken and mobilize the masses against their rulers, was thought to be the ultimate liberator.'[72] The US State Department seriously asked Twitter to postpone a scheduled maintenance on its site in June 2009 so that the Iranian revolution could proceed as hoped for, and Twitter complied (though the revolution didn't). By the end of that year there was a serious campaign to award the Nobel Peace Prize to 'The Internet'. Morozov wrote that the 'faith' of the cyber-utopians

> is not the result of a careful examination of how the Internet is being used by dictators or how it is changing the culture of resistance and dissent. On the contrary, most often it's just unthinking acceptance of conventional wisdom, which posits that since authoritarian governments are censoring the Internet, they must be really afraid of it. Thus, according to this view, the very presence of a vibrant Internet culture greatly increases the odds that such regimes will collapse.[73]

The regimes, in fact, responded to the West's ignorant exaggerations about Twitter by cracking down on Internet freedom. The myth of the liberating apps, nonetheless, carried on for several more years. In a TED talk in February 2013, U2 singer Bono said that the idea of human equality had first been brought to Egypt in ancient times by the Jewish people with their holy book, and that it was brought to Egypt again in 2011 by 'another book, Facebook' (in which Bono had long been a prominent investor).[74] Five months after Bono's talk, Egypt's Muslim Brotherhood government fell to a military coup.

In fairness, Morozov's was scarcely the only voice raised against cyber-utopian myth-making and conventional wisdom five or six years ago. Nonetheless, the shift from optimism to anxiety has been striking, with millions of words thrown over the last year or two at the frightening politics of online subcultures, from ISIS to the alt-right. Meanwhile, it appears the alt-right itself constitutes its politics partly as a response to the leftish online subculture that it dubs 'social justice warriors'.[75] Insofar, it seems, as activists on both sides come out of their 'filter bubbles' long enough to interact at all, it's merely to abuse and caricature each other – with each side feeding off the other's negativity – rather than to deliberate democratically.

But is social networking online really bereft of any emancipatory potential, just because Mark Zuckerberg owns our profiles, or because we're stuck in silos with people who share our politics? Isn't there evidence that, however they sap the energies of people involved in existing movements, Twitter, Facebook and other platforms do actually help to create popular movements in response to events? You need only look at #BlackLivesMatter, #metoo and (closer to home) #Right2Water and #HomeSweet Home to find pertinent examples of important social-media-based campaigns in which oppressed people broke traditional barriers to dissemination of experiences and ideas. Surely it's not implausible to imagine what Eugenia Siapera calls a 'new ontology of the citizen, brought into being through digital acts'.[76]

It's hopeful, perhaps, that one of the most probing critics of net-based social-media relations, Jodi Dean, has in some of her most recent writing constructed social media as a site of struggle rather than simply of exploitation. This is, it seems to me, an important departure, insofar as it tempers the sense of inescapable capitalist capture of our online lives that permeates her earlier vision; it thus brings her, already an important guiding light for this book, closer to some of my own strategic thinking (though I will tease out some remaining differences later). It is worth recalling that in writings starting over a decade ago, culminating in a 2009 book, Dean coined the phrase that has stuck as the perfect critical-theory put-down of the age of social media: 'communicative capitalism'.[77] In this reckoning, all our online 'participation', whatever its ostensible politics, is just grist to capital's mill. Not only are we turned into the unpaid producers of content that provides the medium for profitable advertising, but we are also lured into a sense that politics is easily performed, only ever a like, a retweet or a share away, and that community is something you signal with a hashtag. As critical scholars summarising Dean have written, it is a culture that easily 'descends into "clicktivism", signing online petitions, writing dissenting blogs, sending political tweets', activities that, for all their superficial resistance, end up supporting liberal 'rhetorics of access, participation and democracy, work[ing] ideologically to secure the technological infrastructure of neoliberalism'.[78]

There is an interesting theoretical argument to be had about what form of capital accumulation is happening when Facebook rakes in the money. Is this 'primitive' (or 'original') accumulation, essentially the private enclosure of some thing or things that were previously held in common (the Internet, human sociability) for the extraction of value, something we might call 'rent'? Or is it exploitation, the expropriation of surplus value from the labour of workers, the normal Marxian understanding of 'profit'? (Kylie Jarrett has proposed a fascinating feminist transcendence of this dichotomy by reference to 'the Digital Housewife', a concept that highlights the long history of important, subjectively rich and quasi-voluntary unpaid work.) Although Dean writes about our communications being 'enclosed in circuits as raw materials', she has largely opted for the exploitation model: ordinary people 'working' on social media and someone else profiting from our unpaid labour.[79]

As discussed above, some few 'social influencers' are in fact earning money directly from their Facebook, Twitter, Snapchat and Instagram posts. Since those earnings do not as a rule cut into the profits of the social media platforms but come from sponsors elsewhere, they don't constitute a reconfiguring of the basic exploitative relation – they don't amount to successful class struggle.

In a powerfully optimistic section of her 2016 book *Crowds and Party*, Dean makes it clear why she sees such super-exploited information proletarians, potentially billions of us, as a potentially transformative class in conflict – if not necessarily in direct conflict, yet, with those who exploit us. I am going to look closely at what Dean is saying here, because it's perhaps the most engaging, audacious effort I've seen at making coherent meaning of the global upheavals of the last decade – a meaning that is directly relevant to my own book's mission to distil some radical political agency from the confusion of contemporary communication without resort

to the implausible concept of the public sphere. Looking at the demographics of protesting crowds and riots
around the world, from Occupy Wall Street to Chilean
student risings, from the Arab Spring to the Greek anti-
austerity struggle, from Turkey's Gezi Park to Brazil
rioting against FIFA, Dean sees 'protests of the class of
those proletarianized under communicative capitalism
... They are fronts in global communicative capitalism's
class war, revolts of those whose communicative activities generate value that is expropriated from them.'[80] The
protesters – young, educated, un- and under-employed
– are precisely the people most likely to be giving away
the largest chunks of their efforts and lives to big data:

> This is the real face of the knowledge class ... They
> make more and get less, intensifying inequality with
> every communicative contribution and its trace. A
> 2014 World Economic Forum report puts it blunt-
> ly: 'the greater the role that data play in the global
> economy, the less the majority of individuals will be
> worth.'[81]

Moreover, she says, 'there has been a wide array of
strikes and actions by others we might think of as proletarianized communicative laborers'. A rather hopeful
roll call of strikes in recent years follows, with Dean
insisting, with just a hint of caution, that 'it points to
the active, ongoing, but still disconnected struggles in
the workplaces of communicative laborers'. Ultimately,
however, given the changes in the global information

economy and the weakness of unions, we 'should not expect class struggle in communicative capitalism to manifest primarily as workplace struggles. Communicative production takes place throughout the social field.'[82]

This, then, is the key insight from Dean: we are producing for communicative capitalism all the time, all over the place, not just in traditional workplaces. Struggles that appear to be diverse and diffuse – in relation to debt, to cutbacks, to housing, to education, and so on – are actually comprehensible 'in terms of the class politics of those encountering proletarianization, not as separate and specific issue-based politics'. Moreover, if Occupy takes over a square or Turkish radicals make a park into a site of struggle, they are acting out class struggle in what is effectively the site of communicative production, and if they are pulling out their smartphones to upload images and video and to send out social media messages, then 'Phones are means of production. When they occupy, communicating activists put these means of production to a use of their own choosing, not capital's (although capital can still expropriate their content and metadata).'[83]

Dean has been an implacable opponent of public-sphere theory as a model and ideal for political activity in a networked age.[84] She might nonetheless be accused, at first glance, of having drawn a picture that looks just a little like one an up-to-date Habermasian might recognise: a public sphere that is diverse, plural and located all over the social field, but one that recognises the political as the ultimate and most socially unifying communicative form. For Habermas himself, indeed, the acknowledgement and embrace of complexity and pluralism has been at the centre of defending and re-cuperating a notion of the public sphere that can be relevant in the twenty-first century. As a recent scholarly summary explains: 'Habermas has moved away from a commitment to a singular conception of the bourgeois public sphere so as to recognise a plurality of public spheres.' The public sphere, moreover, can be seen as simply 'the consequence of certain forms of communica-tion, wherever and whenever they take place'. This rather reconfigured public sphere, then, 'is inevitably dispersed, and its legitimacy rests less in the nature of the place where communication occurs and instead in the nature of the communication itself'. Habermas has given way also to the proliferation of identity politics as part of the constitution of the new, improved public sphere: 'instead of deliberation ideally resulting in consensus and a sovereign public, Habermas now embraces the contested nature of public life, the importance of recog-nition of diverse identities and, therefore, the legitimacy of multiple forms and sites of deliberation'.[85]

All that is well and good. A theory that attempted to account for twenty-first-century communication, polit-ical and otherwise, but couldn't begin to describe the fact of its multiplicity, diversity and decentralisation wouldn't be much of a theory at all. Nonetheless, the ac-ceptance of pluralism as a characteristic of contemporary media interactions doesn't change the central difference between Dean and the Habermasians: Dean's model is based not on consensus but on contest, not on deliberation but on conflict. Her hope is not for some sort of restoration of democracy, but for revolutionary change based on the interests of that expropriated proletariat. We are back, again, to hegemony, and the ineradicability of antagonism.

Moreover, even while we give the Habermasians some credit for keeping up with the times, and whatever our feelings about the public sphere, we must be wary of presenting pluralism as though it were a legitimising virtue of the current information order, as opposed to merely an inescapable feature of its technological form. For one thing, we over estimate it: Google News, for instance, 'gives priority weighting to news providers with scale, volume and those who cover topics that are widely covered elsewhere', that is, usually corporate 'legacy'-media companies.[86] The fake-news kerfuffle has strengthened pressure on Google and Facebook to lead us down traditional news paths. As noted in Section 1, what we 'enjoy' online, so far, is at best pluralism without power. We have access to a diversity of viewpoints, but the same ones end up being employed in the setting of policy nationally and internationally practically all the time. 'Even acknowledging the explosion of counter-publicity in a digital age does not necessarily translate into counter-public spheres', Fenton writes, 'if the point at which [what Habermas calls] "the balance of power between civil society and the political systems shifts" is never reached.'[87] Pluralism is, of course, a virtue worthy of rhetorical appeal in certain circumstances: for example, if a state intends to outlaw certain perspectives, or if a national broadcaster consistently ignores a set of popular political positions. In those circumstances of constraint, we should demand pluralism, loudly and clearly. But we should understand its limits and dangers, even as a rhetorical device in the normal operation of communication overload. As Kari Karppinen writes, 'it is becoming even less clear in which sense it is meaningful to speak of media pluralism, if the media landscape is characterised more by abundance and limitless choice than by scarcity or lack of options.'[88]

Getting overexcited about pluralistic choice often means, as we saw in Section 1 in relation to the public sphere itself, simultaneously drawing a veil of mystification across the operation of power. Understanding 'the continuing centrality of questions of power in media politics' – that is to say, looking at the political economy of the media – and enumerating the inequalities and expropriations that those questions reveal should provide some immunity to what Karppinen calls 'the rationalistic idealisations of deliberative democracy' and the public sphere. 'Unequal relations of power', he writes, 'remain crucial in the field of media policy and media institutions and there is no reason to think that technological or any other developments will lead to spontaneous harmony.'[89] As Dean points out, any optimism about the wonders of a pluralistic democratic public sphere in the Internet age has got a certain empirical problem: 'Why, at a time when the means of communication have been revolutionized, when people can contribute their own opinions and access those of others rapidly and immediately, why has democracy failed as a political form?'[90] There is no escaping the fact that media activity, and activism to democratise media, are severely limited tools for building better politics. There is no escaping the need for action that, rather than seeking to improve the messages we get and receive, instead directly challenges power.

As Natalie Fenton observes, just because we have 'power to' doesn't mean we have 'power over'. I can tweet a cutting putdown to @realDonaldTrump, but, short of massive, as-yet-unseen resistance from US government employees, only a federal judge can shoot down his immigration ban. Fenton writes:

the tendency in public sphere frameworks to elide pluralism with communicative freedom ... runs the risk of reducing power to an individual resource that is purely relational and behavioural, and one that will always overemphasize technology to the detriment of social, political and economic context. Democracy conceived of as access to a range of communication and information can only ever take us so far. Pluralism, as a value and set of practices, poses no threat to the neoliberal discourses that can be seen as a powerful and largely successful attempt to reshape the direction of travel of the political for a whole generation, normalizing the individualizing subjectivities that saturate much life and action online, even though this may be constantly under challenge. Pluralism does not automatically transcend global capitalism, and communicative freedom is not a given, even in the digital age.[91]

That hoary old maxim that calls upon radicals to 'speak truth to power' is meaningless if power doesn't fear the truth. 'Claims that the starting conditions for social and political action have been radically changed by digital communications are difficult to take seriously', Fenton writes, 'when they rely solely on the creative autonomy of the individual and largely ignore how these individuals are themselves situated in particular social orders that enable some social and/or political responses and disable others.'[92]

And yet ... something *is* happening here, but we don't (yet) know what it is. While it's highly unlikely that we are going to stop using Facebook and Google en masse, the wider political struggles developing online and on the streets may be, as Dean suggests, the real means to re-appropriate their power over our labour and data. That our tweets are going to somehow move the consensus and change policy in the public sphere for the better are nearly nil, but we are building subversive discourses and transversal alliances in the spaces that the system has left for us. We, as radicals, are making our own politics, not seeking 'constructive debate' and consensus with those who wield all the power.

As discussed in previous sections, we won't achieve any of those political goals by isolating ourselves in towers of chaste political virtue. Strategic engagement with mainstream media and rhetorical appeals to its highest values do have a place in building radical alternative politics. Some of the British scholars whose work has been so valuable to my own study – researchers such as Natalie Fenton and Des Freedman, in particular – are themselves involved in media-critical coalitions such as Hacked Off and the Media Reform Campaign. These groups can get quite a lot of public traction by highlighting how newspapers and broadcasters fail to live up to their own stated, high-modernist values. Sometimes, in newspapers with a particularly high public commitment to those values, the campaigners can even get their own opinion articles printed. (Many Irish radicals who have long suffered from *Guardian*-envy as we gazed at the best of those English daily newspapers have probably been cured of that affliction by seeing how that newspaper opposed and attacked left-wing Labour Party leader Jeremy Corbyn.) They are using the small spaces in the mainstream to elaborate fundamental critiques that can be developed, with growing audiences, elsewhere. One group of London scholars, for example, opted for a quick online publication of their critical study of press coverage of Corbyn,[93] the sort of thing Irish academics should really be doing in relation to media treatment of Sinn Féin and the left-wing parties. This tactical approach is, it seems to me, the embodiment of a smart and sophisticated understanding of hegemony. Hegemony does not mean total control, but rather describes an ongoing dynamic process that offers opportunities for contestation and lots of differences in individuals' political consciousness, even when it does not offer opportunities for revolution. We could do with similar engagement from radical media scholars and practitioners here in Ireland. Arguably, it's more constructive than the periodic talk that percolates among radical and labour activists about developing a new left-wing newspaper for the Irish market.

Freedman himself has recently conceptualised his strategic and theoretical understanding of the media with what he calls a 'contradiction paradigm'. It is, Freedman writes,

> an approach to media power that emphasizes structure and agency, contradiction and action, consensus and conflict; an analytical framework that recognizes the existence of unequal power frameworks but acknowledges that they are not forever frozen; and a perspective that takes seriously the activities of producers and audiences while recognizing the existence of uneven consciousness.[94]

This paradigm might sound like it simply contains multitudes, but its 'contradictions' are usefully dialectical. It offers an alternative to visions of media as an efficient brainwasher as much as it does to recent versions of the public sphere optimistically animated by tech-driven pluralism. Or, to put it another way, it finds a meeting place between the cold, hard, material facts of a political-economy approach to the media and the more fluid understanding of the subjectivity of 'prosumption' that draws on cultural studies' interest in audience agency and the modes of resistance that can reside within, or close to, centres of power. So, yes, of course, it is essential to insist that

> power has to be understood in relation to its material configuration in specific political and economic contexts. In a capitalist society, the media are answerable to the fundamental requirements of capital accumulation and commodity production and function as vital ideological sources of reinforcement for the current economic order.[95]

That goes as much for Google and Facebook as it does for the newspapers and broadcasters owned by Rupert Murdoch and Denis O'Brien. Such a political-economy approach means we don't lose sight of the damage done 'by private ownership and unaccountable state coordination of the media', and that we work 'to identify the institutional, organizational and textual means through which social control is reproduced'.[96] But it's also part of the dynamic nature of capitalist hegemony that the hegemonic system has cracks and fissures, among which can be found the media's own legitimating myths and belief systems. Freedman calls on radical actors 'to reveal and act on the instability and contingency of existing forms of media control', and says this contradiction paradigm offers 'the most persuasive account of how best to challenge the traditions, institutions and practices that underpin it'.[97]

Like any good radical theory, the contradiction paradigm offers a programme for action rather than just for analysis – the point, as always, being not merely to understand the world but to change it, with the help of a framework that identifies systemic points of vulnerability. As Freedman writes, 'Media power, according to this perspective, may be comprehensive but it is nevertheless always unstable and contestable.' The contestation, then, is theory in action – what Antonio Gramsci called the philosophy of praxis.

Gramsci was himself a journalist, as well as an activist and intellectual. His praxis meant that when, for example, he was faced with workers who insisted on buying bourgeois newspapers, he didn't merely chide them for falling for the bosses' propaganda; he offered the workers, knowing the attachment they had formed to the product, a newspaper of their own. His political-economy analysis of the relation of the bourgeois press to the average worker, published in *Avanti!* in 1916, was both merciless and timeless; it could be describing the *Irish Independent*'s relation to the Irish Citizen Army, or to your Sky subscription today:

> the bourgeois newspaper (whatever its hue) is an instrument of struggle motivated by ideas and interests that are contrary to his. Everything that is published is influenced by one idea: that of serving

the dominant class, and which is ineluctably translated into a fact: that of combating the laboring class. And in fact, from the first to the last line the bourgeois newspaper smells of and reveals this preoccupation.

But the beautiful – that is the ugly – thing is this: that instead of asking for money from the bourgeois class to support it in its pitiless work in its favor, the bourgeois newspapers manage to be paid by ... the same laboring classes that they always combat. And the laboring class pays; punctually, generously.

Hundreds of thousands of workers regularly and daily give their pennies to the bourgeois newspapers, thus assisting in creating their power.[98]

Gramsci also offers a devastatingly familiar content analysis of the columns of that bourgeois press:

And so every day this same worker is able to person-ally see that the bourgeois newspapers tell even the simplest of facts in a way that favors the bourgeois class and damns the working class and its politics. Has a strike broken out? The workers are always wrong as far as the bourgeois newspapers are concerned. Is there a demonstration? The demonstrators are al-ways wrong, solely because they are workers they are always hotheads, rioters, hoodlums. The government passes a law? It's always good, useful and just, even if it's ... not. And if there's an electoral, political or administrative struggle? The best programs and candidates are always those of the bourgeois parties.

And we aren't even talking about all the facts that the bourgeois newspapers either keep quiet about, or travesty, or falsify in order to mislead, delude or maintain in ignorance the laboring public. Despite this, the culpable acquiescence of the worker to the bourgeois newspapers is limitless. We have to react against this and recall the worker to the correct evaluation of reality. We have to say and repeat that the pennies tossed there distractedly into the hands of the newsboy are projectiles granted to a bourgeois newspaper, which will hurl it, at the opportune moment, against the working masses.

If the workers were to be persuaded of this most elementary of truths they would learn to boycott the bourgeois press with the same unity and discipline that the bourgeoisie boycott the newspapers of the workers, that is, the Socialist press.[99]

Anyone who has come this far with this book does not need a lecture now on supporting alternative media. You know that in today's media ecology, it's not as simple as buying *Avanti!* in Turin in 1916. You know that some of the best stories you've clicked lately are in the 'bourgeois press' and maybe you got to them through Facebook, helping its owners to earn the pennies that will be hurled back against the working masses. Maybe you know that among the best professional investigative and radical journalism in the English language today is being produced in *The Intercept*, founded, funded and owned by eBay billionaire Pierre Omidyar; its journalists, such as Glenn Greenwald and Jeremy Scahill, are critical of mainstream journalism, including the routines pursued in the name of objectivity, but nonetheless present their practice in fetching, high-modernist hues: 'The *Intercept* is dedicated to producing fearless, adversarial journalism. We believe journalism should bring transparency and accountability to powerful governmental and corporate institutions, and our journalists have the editorial freedom and legal support to pursue this mission.'[100] In Ireland, the *Dublin Inquirer* is, arguably, doing the best probing reporting on the island, with similar highfalutin professional rhetoric, and a really serious need for your financial support.

It seems inescapable to me that a slick corporate-looking website like *The Intercept* can, despite its billionaire boss, play some small part in afflicting the comfortable and helping to build a real political alternative among the afflicted. It's less obvious that the struggles of the *Dublin Inquirer* can do the same, but that doesn't lessen one's admiration for the effort. The commentary and analysis from the likes of *Jacobin* and a host of other new publications and podcasts are also valuable. Political economy can only tell you so much about the content, and utility, of a given media outlet; the endnotes of this book are replete with solid information drawn from commercial-media sources. There are diverse models for making good media, and more failures than successes. Given that there is not one proven formula for maintaining and improving public information resources, we should hesitate before we pour scorn on the potential of any given outlet simply on the basis of its ownership, or marketing bumf, or affiliations. But while we're tempering our condemnations, taking what we can from a variety of sources and trying to improve them, we should be careful not to let the task of making better media distract us from the more urgent one of making better societies – a task to which media can only contribute so much.

Conclusion

I'm a full-time, well-paid academic and a beneficiary of the idea of academic freedom. When I write a book like this one, it is on balance good for me professionally, not the threat it might be if I were shouting communist slogans from a different height. Still, I don't believe intellectually or in my gut in the ideal of the university; I believe that third-level institutions are, like other institutions in societies such as ours, expressions of capitalist class relations, and if I were in any doubt on that point I need look no further than the pay and conditions of other workers in my institute. I believe the (limited, but real) autonomy I enjoy should be the rule rather than the exception in all workplaces. Nonetheless, despite my scepticism about the university ideal, if a threat from my employers against myself, my colleagues or my principles were to materialise, I would not hesitate to combat it with all available tools, including the toney language of Cardinal John Henry Newman's high-Victorian *Idea of a University*, if I thought it would help. I would, in short, demand that fatally flawed institutions live up to their dishonest hype, as part of a way of moving toward better institutions in a better kind of society.

I feel similarly about the public sphere. One of my favourite song and album titles is Funkadelic's *Free Your Mind ... And Your Ass Will Follow*. However, I think there's a little extra activity needed in the middle, where George Clinton put the ellipsis. We break from a conception of the consensual, deliberative public sphere to free our minds, but, having understood the ineradicability of antagonism, perhaps we strategically appeal to some of the hegemonic norms of democracy, freedom and plural-ism that are associated with the public sphere to improve the chances that our many asses will eventually follow.

This is, in the age of a renascent right wing, not just an academic point. If a Le Pen, a Trump or a May were to attack press freedom by, say, jailing a *Le Figaro*, *Washington Post* or *Daily Telegraph* journalist, I would be among the first people, I promise, tweeting quotes from Thomas Jefferson. (This is far from a remote possibility given trends in espionage laws in various jurisdictions.) However, our activity cannot stop there, at the crisis point, but must go deeper, to a critique of communica-tive capitalism, knowing and stating, for example, that the British press has abused the idea of press freedom as a charter for lies and infringement of human rights. As Robin D.G. Kelley writes about the black-radical 'freedom schools' of the 1960s, they 'challenged the myth that the civil rights movement was just about claiming a place in mainstream society. They didn't want equal opportunity in a burning house; they wanted to build a new house.'[100] Even while we battle against the right with the help of liberal norms, we need to make it clear that we don't, ultimately, want to live in the liberals' house. Any strategic appeal, therefore, to the concept of the public sphere must be clearly understood as temporary, contingent and provisional.

Thus, we may seek to occupy the fissures in neoliberal hegemony by attaching ourselves to some of its norms while maintaining the coherence of our critique. The latter requirement, for critical coherence, means not getting dragged into, for example, defence of the wonders of a unitary, inclusive public sphere where everyone gets exposed to the same range of competing ideas when we have simply and correctly weighed in to support the proper funding of a public broadcaster, such as RTÉ. You *can* have one without the other. Unfortunately, at least nine times out of ten, such pro-public-sphere arguments, Natalie Fenton writes, 'are framed by a particular understanding of democracy that accepts the institutional structures of representational politics and applies a liberal pluralism model of democratic practice inherent in Habermasian thought'.[101] Political institutions, in that understanding, are basically meeting their democratic obligations so long as they appear to present options to voters.

The more subtle and dispersed public-sphere vision of the later Habermas, described in Section 3, still doesn't get us past a fundamental problem: that it seeks to serve a democracy that is arguably no longer functional in most Western states, and then hides that democratic failure behind a media-centric concern with communication flows. Anyone who has ever seen a student essay that tries to use the concept of 'deliberative democracy' to describe an individual's interaction with a mobile news app can tell you that it is not a pretty sight. Nonetheless, as testified by the many studies that continue to associate the mere consumption of hard political news with civic virtue, at least implicitly, it is easier to do research on relatively passive media interactions than to get a handle on the complexity of political activity in the social-media environment.

For better or worse, for people who get their politics on Facebook, the prospect of rational, united and common political purpose, in which we move toward consensus through civilised debate, fades further and further into ridiculousness. (The only thing even more ridiculous, with all due respect to Habermas himself, is the idea that we can reconstitute it at European level.) My Facebook feed – which I have probably checked on average every 100 words throughout the writing of this book – bears only scant resemblance to my wife's, let alone a student's or a daughter's or a friend's or a stranger's. We each get different news, each argue about different things, each like different cat videos. I don't mourn the democratic public sphere, because I think it never existed to begin with, but it's particularly ill-equipped as a concept for social and political life today.

This is not the same as saying that our choices for how we organise our collective political expressions boil down to either Habermas or Facebook. Facebook's version of politics clearly can't equip us politically and intellectually for the troubled times that undoubtedly lie ahead. For one thing, genuine democracy requires time.[102] It's merely to say that any theoretical construct that does not and cannot account for Facebook's version of politics is hardly going to be much use as a tool either of description or of action. The political model we need now, writes Jodi Dean, 'is not rooted in figuring out the best sorts of procedures and decision rules for political deliberation. Instead it acknowledges in advance the endless, morphing variety of tools and tactics.' When we assess those tactics, she adds, the crucial question 'is whether they open up opportunities for contestation'.[103] No contest, no politics.

Dean herself, however, believes that the sort of hegemonic public-sphere norms that I hope can be, despite their taint, attached to our critique – 'inclusivity, equality, transparency, and rationality' – have to be abandoned, 'if only to realize them'. In her view, 'they have been coopted by a communicative capitalism that has turned them into their opposite'.[104] This is consistent with Dean's larger political strategy, which also tends to reject conceptions such as 'democracy' and 'left populism'. In this respect, I differ from her and adhere rather to the strategic bloc-building optimism, and indeed populism, of Laclau and Mouffe. My own conception of how counter-hegemony works draws freely on theirs, and involves the building of new alliances and political work that attempts to shift the borders of a looming contest, rather than preparing for old battles across old trenches; for me, this suggests that the norms themselves are contestable, open to recapture, and therefore, for the most part, don't need to be abandoned. I would go so far as to say that this could apply, albeit with highly critical provisionality, to the occasional use of the term 'public sphere' itself. Indeed, with the newly risen right already shifting political boundaries, the movements to resist it building new alliances, and a widespread understanding across Western societies that consensus is weakened and a contest is on, it seems to me that at least some of those norms are there for the taking. You don't need to believe in the public sphere to understand that radicals should claim our space, stand our ground, and seek opportunities to expand; such claiming, standing and expanding are not primarily questions of terminology but of action, and we can choose our terms strategically on the basis of whether they help us act.

I am, nonetheless, sympathetic to a healthy intellectual suspicion of anything that resembles the uncritical   embrace of those normative ideas that have been captured by neoliberalism, especially in the new context where dreamy echoes of liberal idealism are already both a scourge and a temptation. In the US, Democratic Party opponents of Trumpism have been, in a single absurd breath, defending liberty, equality and the CIA. Resistance, to Trumpism and beyond, 'should not rest on venerating an ideal democracy we have never really achieved'.[105] That is why the norms we use must be consistently employed to offer solid and specific critiques of capitalism – for example, by insisting with Wolfgang Streeck that capitalism is clearly now incompatible with democracy, and we would frankly much rather have the latter than the former.[106]

So though 'media' is what I teach, and what much of this book has focused upon, I agree with Fenton and Gavan Titley that we must 'interrogate liberal democracy' itself 'as a condition of theorizing the role of media therein'.[107] As those authors note, all talk of media as the lifeblood of democracy doesn't help much if the democracy has gone:

> it is all too easy to claim that enhancing democracy primarily or centrally depends on a media solution – more plurality, less concentration, better representation. Of course, all of these concerns are of vital importance, yet when written predominantly from the 'media side' of the equation, they tend to distract our attention away from the broader, shifting context of which they are but a part ... we aim to question the status of guiding ideas saturated in assumptions about how deliberation, representation and democratic politics may work, as representative democracy and the organization and distribution of power shift in ways not registered in these canonical ideas.[108]

Media were not responsible for breaking democracy, though neoliberalism arrived on the scene when high-modernist journalism was at its peak, suggesting perhaps that the fourth estate was the watchdog that didn't bark.

Media, now deeply fractured and mistrusted, also won't fix democracy. But media might leave some space – though probably not a sphere – where we can begin to fix it ourselves.

Notes and References

1. McCabe, a police sergeant who had accused colleagues of a number of wrongdoings, was the victim of an alleged clerical error by a social worker that saw him accused of serious sexual abuse of a child. For the political playing-out of the affair, see Pat Leahy, 'Maurice McCabe: How a Controversy Became a Story about Politics,' *Irish Times*, 18 February 2017, http://www.irishtimes.com/news/ireland/irish-news/maurice-mccabe-how-a-controversy-became-a-story-about-politics-1.2979574.

2. In keeping with the editors' intentions for this series of short books, I have endeavoured to keep notes and citations to a minimum, for a smoother, less academic reading experience. I hope, nonetheless, that my borrowings are clear and credited, and may point readers in some useful directions.

3. Philip Bobbitt, 'Injunctions Protect the Public Sphere', *Guardian*, 2 May 2011, http://www.theguardian.com/comment isfree/2011/may/02/injunctions-media-public-andrew-marr.

4. Wikipedia contributors, 'Public Sphere', Wikipedia, The Free Encyclopedia, 13 January 2017, https://en.wikipedia.org/w/index.php?title=Public_sphere&oldid=759914944.

5. Thomas Jefferson, 'Amendment I (Speech and Press): Thomas Jefferson to Edward Carrington, 16 January 1787', http://press-pubs.uchicago.edu/founders/documents/amendI_speechs8.html (accessed 5 February 2017).

6. Jürgen Habermas, *The Structural Transformation of the Public Sphere: An Inquiry Into a Category of Bourgeois Society* (Cambridge, MA: MIT Press, 1991), pp. 41–2.

7. Michael Schudson, 'A Family of Public Spheres', Social Science Research Council, 4 August 2009. http://publicsphere.ssrc.org/schudson-a-family-of-public-spheres/ (accessed 5 February 2017). See also Stacy Clifford Simplican, *The Capacity Contract: Intellectual Disability and the Question of Citizenship* (London: University of Minnesota Press, 2015) for a fascinating reflection on how intellectual difference and disability challenge such concepts of deliberative democracy.

8. Daniel C. Hallin, 'The Passing of the "High Modernism" of American Journalism', *Journal of Communication*, vol. 42, no. 3 (1 September 1992), pp. 14–25.

9. Doug Underwood, *When MBAs Rule the Newsroom: How Markets and Managers Are Shaping Today's Media* (New York: Columbia University Press, 1993); Nick Davies, *Flat Earth News: An Award-winning Reporter Exposes Falsehood, Distortion and Propaganda in the Global Media* (London: Chatto & Windus, 2008); Robert McChesney and John Nichols, *The Death and Life of American Journalism: The Media Revolution That Will Begin the World Again* (New York: Nation Books, 2011).

10. Daniel C. Hallin, 'Neoliberalism, Social Movements and Change in Media Systems in the Late Twentieth Century', in David Hesmondhalgh and Jason Toynbee (eds), The Media and Social Theory, (London: Routledge, 2008), p. 55.

11. Nick Couldry, *Why Voice Matters: Culture and Politics After Neoliberalism* (London: SAGE, 2010), pp. 84, 86.

12. Razmig Keucheyan, *The Left Hemisphere: Mapping Critical Theory Today*, trans. Gregory Elliott (London: Verso Books, 2013), p. 138.

13. The Economist, 'Do Social Media Threaten Democracy?' *The Economist* (4 Nov, 2017), https://www.economist.com/news/

leaders/21730871-facebook-google-and-twitter-were-supposed-save-politics-good-information-drove-out.

14. Deborah Cook, 'The Talking Cure in Habermas's Republic', *New Left Review*, 12 (2001), no. 136.

15. Jürgen Habermas, 'How To Pull the Ground From Under Right-wing Populism', *Social Europe*, 17 November 2016, https://www.socialeurope.eu/2016/11/democratic-polarisation-pull-ground-right-wing-populism/.

16. Stathis Kouvelakis, 'Syriza's Rise and Fall', *New Left Review*, no. 97 (January–February 2016): p. 54.

17. For my own book-length consideration of one such phenomenon, see *The Frontman: Bono (In the Name of Power)* (London: Verso Books, 2013).

18. Ernesto Laclau and Chantal Mouffe, *Hegemony and Socialist Strategy: Towards a Radical Democratic Politics* (London: Verso Books, 2001), pp. xvi–xvii.

19. Ibid. p. xvii.

20. Ibid. p. xviii.

21. Wolfgang Streeck, *How Will Capitalism End?* (London: Verso Books, 2016), p. 94.

22. Chantal Mouffe, 'The Populist Moment', *openDemocracy*, 21 November 2016, https://www.opendemocracy.net/democraciaabierta/chantal-mouffe/populist-moment.

23. The works of Wolfgang Streeck (cited above), Wendy Brown and the late Irish political scientist Peter Mair provide probably the best guide to neoliberalism's destruction of democracy. For the latter two, see, for example Wendy Brown, 'Neo-Liberalism and the End of Liberal Democracy', *Theory & Event*, vol. 7, no. 1 (2003), doi:10.1353/tae.2003.0020; Wendy Brown, 'The End of Educated Democracy', *Representations*, vol. 116, no. 1 (November

2011), pp. 19–41; Peter Mair, *Ruling the Void: The Hollowing out of Western Democracies* (London: Verso Books, 2013).

24. Natalie Fenton, *Digital, Political, Radical* (Cambridge: Polity Press, 2016), Chapter 3.

25. Ibid. Chapter 1.

26. Patrick E. Tyler, 'Threats and Responses: News Analysis A New Power in the Streets', *New York Times*, 17 February 2003, https://www.nytimes.com/2003/02/17/world/threats-and-responses-news-analysis-a-new-power-in-the-streets.html. Ishaan Tharoor, 'Viewpoint: Why Was the Biggest Protest in World History Ignored?', *Time*, 15 February 2013, http://world.time.com/2013/02/15/viewpoint-why-was-the-biggest-protest-in-world-history-ignored/.

27. John Berger, 'The Nature of Mass Demonstrations', *CounterPunch*, 20 January 2017, http://www.counterpunch.org/2017/01/20/the-nature-of-mass-demonstrations/.

28. Ibid.

29. The article eventually appeared on a US website: Harry Browne, 'Shannon Warport, "No More Business as Usual"', *CounterPunch*, 3 December 2003, http://www.counterpunch.org/2003/12/03/shannon-warport-quot-no-more-business-as-usual-quot/.

30. Cook, 'The Talking Cure in Habermas's Republic', p. 147.

31. Gavan Titley, 'The Debatability of Racism: Networked Participative Media and Postracialism', *Rasismista Ja Rajoista*, 17 February 2016, https://raster.fi/2016/02/17/the-debatability-of-racism-networked-participative-media-and-postracialism/.

32. Ryan Gallagher, 'Ten Revelations From Bradley Manning's WikiLeaks Documents', *Slate Magazine*, 4 June 2013, http://www.slate.com/blogs/future_tense/2013/06/04/bradley_manning_trial_10_revelations_from_wikileaks_documents_on_iraq_afghanistan.html.

33. Mark Fisher, 'Exiting the Vampire Castle', *North Star*, 22 November 2013, http://www.thenorthstar.info/?p=11299.

34. '2017 Edelman Trust Barometer – Global Results', *Edelman*, 12. Accessed 9 February 2017. http://www.edelman.com/global-results/; Colin Coyle, 'Naughten Acts on Drop in RTÉ Trust', *Sunday Times* (Irish Edition), 12 February 2017, http://www.thetimes.co.uk/article/naughten-acts-on-drop-in-rte-trust-l7k8z7z8r.

35. Quoted in Paul Jones, *Raymond Williams' Sociology of Culture: A Critical Reconstruction* (Houndmills: Palgrave Macmillian, 2006), p. 109.

36. For a good summary of the Hallin spheres and a consideration of their relevance in the Internet age, see Jay Rosen, 'Audience Atomization Overcome: Why the Internet Weakens the Authority of the Press', *PressThink*, 12 January 2009, http://archive.pressthink.org/2009/01/12/atomization.html.

37. Martin J. Power, Amanda Haynes and Eoin Devereux, 'Reasonable People vs. The Sinister Fringe: Interrogating the Framing of Ireland's Water Charge Protestors through the Media Politics of Dissent', *Critical Discourse Studies*, vol. 13, no. 3 (2016), pp. 261–77; Julien Mercille, *The Political Economy and Media Coverage of the European Economic Crisis: The Case of Ireland* (London: Routledge, 2014).

38. Rory Hearne, 'The Irish Water War, Austerity and the "Risen People"', 20 April 2015, https://www.maynoothuniversity.ie/sites/default/files/assets/document/TheIrishWaterwar_0.pdf.

39. See Henry Silke, 'An Attack on Democracy', *Critical Media Review*, 9 February 2015, https://criticalmediareview.wordpress.com/2015/02/09/an-attack-on-democracy/.

40. I am grateful to my co-authors Colin Coulter, Gavan Titley, Vanessa Hetherington and Roddy Flynn. Some of what follows below has not been previously published, while other elements

have appeared in Colin Coulter et al., '"These People Protesting Might Not Be So Strident If Their Own Jobs Were on the Line": Representations of the "Economic Consequences" of Opposition to the Iraq War in the Irish National Press', *Media, War & Conflict*, vol. 9, no. 2 (1 August 2016): pp. 113–36. Document research was funded by the Joseph Rowntree Charitable Trust.

41. Julian Gottlieb, 'Protest News Framing Cycle: How the *New York Times* Covered Occupy Wall Street', *International Journal of Communication Systems*, no. 9 (15 January 2015), pp. 231–53; Francis L.F. Lee, 'Triggering the Protest Paradigm: Examining Factors Affecting News Coverage of Protests', *International Journal of Communication Systems*, no. 8 (14 August 2014), pp. 2725–46; Michael P. Boyle, Douglas M. McLeod and Cory L. Armstrong, 'Adherence to the Protest Paradigm: The Influence of Protest Goals and Tactics on News Coverage in U.S. and International Newspapers', *International Journal of Press/Politics*, 2 February 2012, doi:10.1177/1940161211433837.

42. A full account of this incident and its long legal aftermath can be found in Harry Browne, *Hammered by the Irish: How the Pitstop Ploughshares Disabled a US Warplane, With Ireland's Blessing* (Petrolia: CounterPunch Books, 2008).

43. The following several paragraphs are based closely on my testimony to the Oireachtas Joint Committee of Inquiry into the Banking Crisis in March 2015.

44. Daniel C. Hallin, 'The Passing of the "High Modernism" of American Journalism Revisited', *Political Communication Report*, vol. 16, no. 1 (2006), http://www.jour.unr.edu/pcr/.

45. Declan Fahy, Mark O'Brien and Valerio Poti, 'From Boom to Bust: A Post-Celtic Tiger Analysis of the Norms, Values and Roles of Irish Financial Journalists', *Irish Communication Review*, no. 12 (2010): p. 15.

46. Ibid. pp. 7–8.

47. Ibid. pp. 13–14.

48. See Underwood, *When MBAs Rule the Newsroom: How Markets and Managers Are Shaping Today's Media*.

49. Michael Bromley, 'The End of Journalism? Changes in Workplace Practices in the Press and Broadcasting in the 1990s', in, Michael Bromley and Tom O'Malley (eds), *A Journalism Reader* (Abingdon: Psychology Press, 1997), 331.

50. Thomas Hanitzsch, 'Deconstructing Journalism Culture: Toward a Universal Theory', *Communication Theory*, vol. 17, no. 4 (1 November 2007) 374.

51. David Harvey, *A Brief History of Neoliberalism* (Oxford: Oxford University Press, 2005), p. 42.

52. James Curran, 'The Future of Journalism', *Journalism Studies* 11, no. 4 (2010): 469.

53. Fintan O'Toole, 'Denis O'Brien's Influence and the Meaning of Press Freedom', *Irish Times*, 9 June 2015, http://www.irishtimes.com/opinion/fintan-o-toole-denis-o-brien-s-influence-and-the-meaning-of-press-freedom-1.2242043.

54. Roderick Flynn, 'Ireland', *Media Pluralism Monitor*, 20 January 2016, http://monitor.cmpf.eui.eu/mpm2015/results/ireland/.

55. See Mark Cullinane, 'Column: RTÉ's Future Plans Are Missing One Vital Ingredient: You', *The Journal.ie*, 29 September 2013, http://www.thejournal.ie/readme/rte-five-year-strategy-analysis-1101778-Sep2013/.

56. Toril Aalberg, 'Does Public Media Enhance Citizen Knowledge? Sifting Through the Evidence', Political Economy Research Centre, Goldsmiths, University of London (2015), p. 6, http://www.perc.org.uk/perc/wp-content/uploads/2015/12/PERC-Paper-13-Public-Media-and-Citizen-Knowledge-Toril-Aalberg-Dec-15.pdf.

57. Peter Murtagh, 'Crime Reporters Object to Negative Image of Their Trade', *Irish Times*, 10 February 2017, http://www.

irishtimes.com/news/crime-and-law/crime-reporters-object-to-negative-image-of-their-trade-1.2970769.

58. For a consideration of some of the problems associated with philanthropic funding of journalism, see Harry Browne, 'Foundation-funded Journalism: Reasons to Be Wary of Charitable Support', *Journalism Studies*, vol. 11, no. 6 (2010), pp. 889–903.

59. Paul Bond, 'Leslie Moonves on Donald Trump: "It May Not Be Good for America, But It's Damn Good for CBS"', *Hollywood Reporter*, 29 February 2016, http://www.hollywoodreporter.com/news/leslie-moonves-donald-trump-may-871464.

60. William Cobbett, *Political Register*, August 1830, in John Simkin, 'William Cobbett', *Spartacus Educational*, http://spartacus-educational.com/PRcobbett.htm (accessed 12 February 2017).

61. James Curran and Jean Seaton, *Power Without Responsibility: Press, Broadcasting and the Internet in Britain* (London: Routledge, 2009), p. 5.

62. Quoted in A.J. Catoline, 'Editing Trump: The Making of a Reality TV Star Who Would Be President – CineMontage', *CineMontage*, 12 October 2016, http://cinemontage.org/2016/10/editing-trump-reality-tv-star-who-would-be-president/.

63. For a reasonably full and frank account of her practice and ethical boundaries from one Irish journalist who has turned to professional 'influencing', see these two posts: Rosemary Mac Cabe, 'Why I Quit My Job – and What's next? – Rosemary Mac Cabe', Rosemary Mac Cabe, 27 May 2016, http://rosemary maccabe.com/why-quit-job-what-next/; Rosemary Mac Cabe, 'Disclaimer – Rosemary Mac Cabe', Rosemary Mac Cabe, http://rosemarymaccabe.com/disclaimer/ (accessed 12 February 2017).

64. Craig Silverman and Lawrence Alexander, 'How Teens In the Balkans Are Duping Trump Supporters With Fake News',

BuzzFeed, 3 November 2016, https://www.buzzfeed.com/craigsilverman/how-macedonia-became-a-global-hub-for-pro-trump-misinfo.

65. Jacob L. Nelson, 'Is "Fake News" a Fake Problem?', *Columbia Journalism Review*, 31 January 2017, http://www.cjr.org/analysis/fake-news-facebook-audience-drudge-breitbart-study.php.

66. Hunt Allcott and Matthew Gentzkow, 'Social Media and Fake News in the 2016 Election', *Stanford.edu*, January 2017, https://web.stanford.edu/~gentzkow/research/fakenews.pdf.

67. Craig Timberg, 'Russian Propaganda Effort Helped Spread "Fake News" During Election, Experts Say', *Washington Post*, 24 November 2016, https://www.washingtonpost.com/business/economy/russian-propaganda-effort-helped-spread-fake-news-during-election-experts-say/2016/11/24/793903b6-8a40-4ca9-b712-716af66098fe_story.html. For one debunking, see Glenn Greenwald, 'WashPost Is Richly Rewarded for False News About Russia Threat While Public Is Deceived', *Intercept*, 4 January 2017, https://theintercept.com/2017/01/04/washpost-is-richly-rewarded-for-false-news-about-russia-threat-while-public-is-deceived/.

68. Des Freedman and Justin Schlosberg, 'Murdoch's Access to British Prime Minister Shows Media Power Still in Hands of the Few', *Conversation*, 2017, http://theconversation.com/murdochs-access-to-british-prime-minister-shows-media-power-still-in-hands-of-the-few-72547.

69. Hannes Grassegger, 'The Data That Turned the World Upside Down', *ZCommunications*, 5 February 2017, https://zcomm.org/znetarticle/the-data-that-turned-the-world-upside-down/.

70. Ibid.

71. Brian O'Neill, J. Ignacio Gallego and Frauke Zeller, 'New Perspectives on Audience Activity: "Prosumption" and Media Activism as Audience Practices', in Kim Christian Schrøder, Nico Carpentier and Laurie Hallett (eds), *Audience Transformations:*

Shifting Audience Positions in Late Modernity, (London: Routledge, 2013), p. 14.

72. Evgeny Morozov, *The Net Delusion: The Dark Side of Internet Freedom* (New York: PublicAffairs, 2011), pp. 3, 6.

73. Ibid. p. 21.

74. Harry Browne, '"Factivism" and Other Fairytales from Bono', *CounterPunch*, 19 March 2013, http://www.counterpunch.org/2013/03/19/factivism-and-other-fairytales-from-bono/.

75. Angela Nagle, 'Angela Nagle: What the Alt-Right Is Really All About', *Irish Times*, 6 January 2017, http://www.irishtimes.com/opinion/angela-nagle-what-the-alt-right-is-really-all-about-1.2926929.

76. Eugenia Siapera, 'Reclaiming Citizenship in the Post-Democratic Condition', *Journal of Citizenship and Globalization Studies*, vol 1, no. 1 (2017): 34.

77. Jodi Dean, *Democracy and Other Neoliberal Fantasies: Communicative Capitalism and Left Politics* (Durham, NC: Duke University Press, 2009).

78. Natalie Fenton and Gavan Titley, 'Mourning and Longing: Media Studies Learning to Let Go of Liberal Democracy', *European Journal of Communication*, vol. 30, no. 5 (11 September 2015), p. 567.

79. Jodi Dean, *Crowds and Party* (London: Verso Books, 2016), p. 16, and Kylie Jarrett, *Feminism, Labour and Digital Media: The Digital Housewife* (London: Routledge, 2015).

80. Ibid.

81. Ibid.

82. Ibid. p. 17.

83. Ibid. p. 18.

84. Jodi Dean, 'Why the Net Is Not a Public Sphere', *Constellations*, vol. 10, no. 1 (2003), pp. 95–112.

85. Peter Lunt and Sonia Livingstone, 'Media Studies' Fascination with the Concept of the Public Sphere: Critical Reflections and Emerging Debates', *Media Culture & Society*, vol. 35, no. 1 (January 17, 2013): p. 92.

86. Freedman and Schlosberg, 'Murdoch's Access to British Prime Minister Shows Media Power Still in Hands of the Few'.

87. Fenton, *Digital, Political, Radical*, Chapter 3.

88. Kari Karppinen, 'Media and the Paradoxes of Pluralism', in David Hesmondhalgh and Jason Toynbee (eds), *The Media and Social Theory*, (London: Routledge, 2008), p. 40.

89. Ibid.

90. Dean, *Democracy and Other Neoliberal Fantasies*, p. 25.

91. Fenton, *Digital, Political, Radical*, Chapter 3.

92. Ibid. Chapter 5.

93. Bart Cammaerts et al., 'Journalistic Representations of Jeremy Corbyn in the British Press: From Watchdog to Attackdog' (Media@LSE, 2016), http://www.lse.ac.uk/media@lse/research/pdf/JeremyCorbyn/Cobyn-Report-FINAL.pdf.

94. Des Freedman, 'Paradigms of Media Power', *Communication, Culture & Critique*, vol. 8, no. 2 (1 June 2015), p. 286.

95. Des Freedman, *The Contradictions of Media Power* (London: Bloomsbury Publishing, 2014), p. 145.

96. Ibid.

97. Ibid. p. 146.

98. Antonio Gramsci, 'Newspapers and the Workers 1916', https://www.marxists.org/archive/gramsci/1916/12/newspapers.htm (accessed 13 February 2017)

99. Ibid.

100. 'About & Contacts – The Intercept', *Intercept*, https://theintercept.com/staff/ (accessed 13 February 2017)

101. Robin D.G. Kelley, 'Black Study, Black Struggle', *Boston Review*, 1 March 2016, http://bostonreview.net/forum/robin-d-g-kelley-black-study-black-struggle.

102. Fenton, *Digital, Political, Radical*, Chapter 2.

103. Veronica Barassi, 'Social Media, Immediacy, and the Time for Democracy: Critical Reflections on Social Media as "Temporalizing Practices"', in Lina Dencik and Oliver Leistert (eds), *Critical Perspectives on Social Media and Protest: Between Control and Emancipation* (London: Rowman & Littlefield International, 2015), pp. 73–88.

104. Dean, 'Why the Net Is Not a Public Sphere', p. 109.

105. Ibid.

106. Thea Riofrancos, 'Democracy Without the People', *n+1*, 6 February 2017, https://nplusonemag.com/online-only/online-only/democracy-without-the-people/.

107. Streeck, *How Will Capitalism End?*

108. Fenton and Titley, 'Mourning and Longing: Media Studies Learning to Let Go of Liberal Democracy', p. 558.

109. Ibid. p. 555.

Bibliography

'2017 Edelman Trust Barometer – Global Results', *Edelman*.
http://www.edelman.com/global-results/(accessed 9 February
2017).

Aalberg, Toril, 'Does Public Media Enhance Citizen Knowledge?
Sifting Through the Evidence', Political Economy Research
Centre, Goldsmiths, University of London, 2015, http://www.
perc.org.uk/perc/wp-content/uploads/2015/12/PERC-Paper-13-
Public-Media-and-Citizen-Knowledge-Toril-Aalberg-Dec-15.pdf.

'About & Contacts – The Intercept', *The Intercept*. https://
theintercept.com/staff/(accessed 13 February 2017).

Allcott, Hunt and Matthew Gentzkow, 'Social Media and Fake
News in the 2016 Election', *Stanford.edu*, January 2017, https://
web.stanford.edu/~gentzkow/research/fakenews.pdf.

Barassi, Veronica, 'Social Media, Immediacy, and the Time
for Democracy: Critical Reflections on Social Media as
"Temporalizing Practices"', in Lina Dencik and Oliver Leistert
(eds), *Critical Perspectives on Social Media and Protest: Between
Control and Emancipation* (London: Rowman & Littlefield
International, 2015), pp. 73–88

Berger, John, 'The Nature of Mass Demonstrations',
CounterPunch, 20 January 2017, http://www.counterpunch.
org/2017/01/20/the-nature-of-mass-demonstrations/.

Bobbitt, Philip, 'Injunctions Protect the Public Sphere,' *Guardian*, 2 May 2011, http://www.theguardian.com/commentisfree/2011/may/02/injunctions-media-public-andrew-marr.

Bond, Paul, 'Leslie Moonves on Donald Trump: "It May Not Be Good for America, but It's Damn Good for CBS"', *Hollywood Reporter*, 29 February 2016, http://www.hollywoodreporter.com/news/leslie-moonves-donald-trump-may-871464.

Boyle, Michael P., Douglas M. McLeod and Cory L. Armstrong, 'Adherence to the Protest Paradigm: The Influence of Protest Goals and Tactics on News Coverage in US and International Newspapers', *International Journal of Press/Politics*, 2 February 2012, doi:10.1177/1940161211433837.

Bromley, Michael, 'The End of Journalism? Changes in Workplace Practices in the Press and Broadcasting in the 1990s,' in Michael Bromley and Tom O'Malley (eds), *A Journalism Reader* (Abingdon: Psychology Press, 1997).

Browne, Harry, '"Factivism" and Other Fairytales From Bono,' *CounterPunch*, 19 March 2013, http://www.counterpunch.org/2013/03/19/factivism-and-other-fairytales-from-bono/.

———. 'Foundation-Funded Journalism: Reasons to Be Wary of Charitable Support', *Journalism Studies*, vol. 11, no. 6 (2010), pp. 889–903.

———. *Hammered by the Irish: How the Pitstop Ploughshares Disabled a US Warplane, With Ireland's Blessing* (Petrolia: CounterPunch Books, 2008).

———. 'Shannon Warport, "No More Business as Usual"', *CounterPunch*, 3 December 2003, http://www.counterpunch.org/2003/12/03/shannon-warport-quot-no-more-business-as-usual-quot/.

———. *The Frontman: Bono (In the Name of Power)* (London: Verso Books, 2013).

Brown, Wendy, 'Neo-Liberalism and the End of Liberal Democracy', *Theory & Event*, vol. 7, no. 1 (2003), doi:10.1353/tae.2003.0020.

————. 'The End of Educated Democracy', *Representations*, vol. 116, no. 1 (November 2011), pp. 19–41.

Cammaerts, Bart, Brooks DeCillia, João Magalhães and César Jimenez-Martínez, 'Journalistic Representations of Jeremy Corbyn in the British Press: From Watchdog to Attackdog', Media@LSE, 2016, http://www.lse.ac.uk/media@lse/research/pdf/JeremyCorbyn/Cobyn-Report-FINAL.pdf.

Catoline, A.J. 'Editing Trump: The Making of a Reality TV Star Who Would Be President – CineMontage', *CineMontage*, 12 October 2016, http://cinemontage.org/2016/10/editing-trump-reality-tv-star-who-would-be-president/.

Cook, Deborah, 'The Talking Cure in Habermas's Republic', *New Left Review*, no. 12 (2001), pp. 135–51.

Couldry, Nick, *Why Voice Matters: Culture and Politics After Neoliberalism* (London: SAGE, 2010).

Coulter, Colin, Harry Browne, Roddy Flynn, Vanessa Hetherington and Gavan Titley, '"These People Protesting Might Not Be so Strident If Their Own Jobs Were On the Line": Representations of the "Economic Consequences" of Opposition to the Iraq War in the Irish National Press', *Media, War & Conflict*, vol. 9, no. 2 (1 August 2016, pp. 113–36.

Coyle, Colin, 'Naughten Acts on Drop in RTÉ Trust', *Sunday Times* (Irish Edition), 12 February 2017, http://www.thetimes.co.uk/article/naughten-acts-on-drop-in-rte-trust-l7k8z7z8r.

Cullinane, Mark, 'Column: RTÉ's Future Plans Are Missing One Vital Ingredient: You', *TheJournal.ie*, 29 September 2013, http://www.thejournal.ie/readme/rte-five-year-strategy-analysis-1101778-Sep2013/.

Curran, James, 'The Future of Journalism', *Journalism Studies*, vol. 11, no. 4 (2010), pp. 464–76.

Curran, James and Jean Seaton, *Power Without Responsibility: Press, Broadcasting and the Internet in Britain* (London: Routledge, 2009).

Economist, The. 'Do Social Media Threaten Democracy?' *The Economist* (4 Nov 2017) https://www.economist.com/news/leaders/21730871-facebook-google-and-twitter-were-supposed-save-politics-good-information-drove-out.

Davies, Nick, *Flat Earth News: An Award-winning Reporter Exposes Falsehood, Distortion and Propaganda in the Global Media* (London: Chatto & Windus, 2008).

Dean, Jodi, *Crowds and Party* (London: Verso Books, 2016).

———. *Democracy and Other Neoliberal Fantasies: Communicative Capitalism and Left Politics* (Durham, NC: Duke University Press, 2009).

———. 'Why the Net Is Not a Public Sphere', *Constellations*, vol. 10, no. 1 (2003), pp. 95–112.

Fahy, Declan, Mark O'Brien and Valerio Poti, 'From Boom to Bust: A Post-Celtic Tiger Analysis of the Norms, Values and Roles of Irish Financial Journalists', *Irish Communication Review*, no. 12 (2010), pp. 5–20.

Fenton, Natalie, *Digital, Political, Radical* (Cambridge: Polity Press, 2016).

Fenton, Natalie and Gavan Titley, 'Mourning and Longing: Media Studies Learning to Let Go of Liberal Democracy', *European Journal of Communication*, vol. 30, no. 5 (11 September 2015), pp. 554–70.

Fisher, Mark, 'Exiting the Vampire Castle', *North Star*, 22 November 2013, http://www.thenorthstar.info/?p=11299.

Flynn, Roderick, 'Ireland', *Media Pluralism Monitor*, 20 January 2016, http://monitor.cmpf.eui.eu/mpm2015/results/ireland/.

Freedman, Des 'Paradigms of Media Power', *Communication, Culture & Critique*, vol. 8, no. 2 (1 June 2015), pp. 273–89.

———. *The Contradictions of Media Power* (London: Bloomsbury, 2014).

Freedman, Des and Justin Schlosberg, 'Murdoch's Access to British Prime Minister Shows Media Power Still in Hands of the Few', *Conversation*, 2017, http://theconversation.com/murdochs-access-to-british-prime-minister-shows-media-power-still-in-hands-of-the-few-72547.

Gallagher, Ryan, 'Ten Revelations From Bradley Manning's WikiLeaks Documents', *Slate Magazine*, 4 June 2013, http://www.slate.com/blogs/future_tense/2013/06/04/bradley_manning_trial_10_revelations_from_wikileaks_documents_on_iraq_afghanistan.html.

Gottlieb, Julian, 'Protest News Framing Cycle: How the New York Times Covered Occupy Wall Street', *International Journal of Communication Systems, no.* 9 (15 January 2015), pp. 231–53.

Gramsci, Antonio, 'Newspapers and the Workers 1916', https://www.marxists.org/archive/gramsci/1916/12/newspapers.htm (accessed 13 February 2017).

Grassegger, Hannes, 'The Data That Turned the World Upside Down', *ZCommunications*, 5 February 2017, https://zcomm.org/znetarticle/the-data-that-turned-the-world-upside-down/.

Greenwald, Glenn, 'WashPost Is Richly Rewarded for False News About Russia Threat While Public Is Deceived', *Intercept*, 4 January 2017, https://theintercept.com/2017/01/04/washpost-is-richly-rewarded-for-false-news-about-russia-threat-while-public-is-deceived/.

Habermas, Jürgen, 'How To Pull The Ground From Under Right-Wing Populism', *Social Europe*, 17 November 2016, https://www.

socialeurope.eu/2016/11/democratic-polarisation-pull-ground-right-wing-populism/.

———. *The Structural Transformation of the Public Sphere: An Inquiry Into a Category of Bourgeois Society* (Cambridge MA: MIT Press, 1991).

Hallin, Daniel C., 'Neoliberalism, Social Movements and Change in Media Systems in the Late Twentieth Century in David Hesmondhalgh and Jason Toynbee (eds), *The Media and Social Theory* (London: Routledge, 2008), pp. 43–58.

———. 'The Passing of the "High Modernism" of American Journalism', *Journal of Communication*, vol. 42, no. 3 (1 September 1992), pp. 14–25.

———. 'The Passing of the "High Modernism" of American Journalism Revisited', *Political Communication Report*, vol. 16, no. 1 (2006), http://www.jour.unr.edu/pcr/.

Hanitzsch, Thomas, 'Deconstructing Journalism Culture: Toward a Universal Theory', *Communication Theory*, vol. 17, no. 4 (1 November 2007), pp. 367–85.

Harvey, David, *A Brief History of Neoliberalism* (Oxford: Oxford University Press, 2005).

Hearne, Rory, 'The Irish Water War, Austerity and the "Risen People"', April 2015, https://www.maynoothuniversity.ie/sites/default/files/assets/document/TheIrishWaterwar_0.pdf.

Jarrett, Kylie, *Feminism, Labour and Digital Media: The Digital Housewife* (London: Routledge, 2015).

Jefferson, Thomas, 'Amendment I (Speech and Press): Thomas Jefferson to Edward Carrington, 16 January 1787', http://press-pubs.uchicago.edu/founders/documents/amendI_speechs8.html, (accessed 5 February 2017)

Jones, Paul, *Raymond Williams' Sociology of Culture: A Critical Reconstruction* (Houndmills: Palgrave Macmillian, 2006).

Karppinen, Kari, 'Media and the Paradoxes of Pluralism', in David Hesmondhalgh and Jason Toynbee (eds), *The Media and Social Theory* (London: Routledge, 2008), pp. 27–42.

Kelley, Robin D.G., 'Black Study, Black Struggle', *Boston Review*, 1 March 2016, http://bostonreview.net/forum/robin-d-g-kelley-black-study-black-struggle.

Keucheyan, Razmig, *The Left Hemisphere: Mapping Critical Theory Today*, trans. Gregory Elliott (London: Verso Books, 2013).

Kouvelakis, Stathis, 'Syriza's Rise and Fall', *New Left Review*, no. 97 (January–February 2016): pp. 45–70.

Laclau, Ernesto and Chantal Mouffe, *Hegemony and Socialist Strategy: Towards a Radical Democratic Politics* (London: Verso, 2001).

Leahy, Pat, 'Maurice McCabe: How a Controversy Became a Story About Politics', *Irish Times*, 18 February 2017, http://www.irishtimes.com/news/ireland/irish-news/maurice-mccabe-how-a-controversy-became-a-story-about-politics-1.2979574.

Lee, Francis L.F., 'Triggering the Protest Paradigm: Examining Factors Affecting News Coverage of Protests', *International Journal of Communication Systems*, vol. 8 (14 August 2014), pp. 2725–46.

Lunt, Peter and Sonia Livingstone, 'Media Studies' Fascination With the Concept of the Public Sphere: Critical Reflections and Emerging Debates', *Media Culture & Society*, vol. 35, no. 1 (17 January 2013), pp. 87–96.

Mac Cabe, Rosemary, 'Disclaimer – Rosemary Mac Cabe', *Rosemary Mac Cabe*. http://rosemarymaccabe.com/disclaimer/ (accessed 12 February 2017).

————. 'Why I Quit My Job – and What's next? – Rosemary Mac Cabe', *Rosemary Mac Cabe*, 27 May 2016, http://rosemarymaccabe.com/why-quit-job-what-next/.

Mair, Peter, *Ruling the Void: The Hollowing out of Western Democracies* (London: Verso Books, 2013).

McChesney, Robert and John Nichols, *The Death and Life of American Journalism: The Media Revolution that Will Begin the World Again*, (New York: Nation Books, 2011).

Mercille, Julien, *The Political Economy and Media Coverage of the European Economic Crisis: The Case of Ireland* (London: Routledge, 2014).

Morozov, Evgeny, *The Net Delusion: The Dark Side of Internet Freedom* (New York: PublicAffairs, 2011).

Mouffe, Chantal, 'The Populist Moment', *openDemocracy*, 21 November 2016, https://www.opendemocracy.net/democraciaabierta/chantal-mouffe/populist-moment.

Murtagh, Peter, 'Crime Reporters Object to Negative Image of Their Trade', *Irish Times*, 10 February 2017, http://www.irishtimes.com/news/crime-and-law/crime-reporters-object-to-negative-image-of-their-trade-1.2970769.

Nagle, Angela, 'What the Alt-Right Is Really All About', *Irish Times*, 6 January 2017, http://www.irishtimes.com/opinion/angela-nagle-what-the-alt-right-is-really-all-about-1.2926929.

Nelson, Jacob L., 'Is "Fake News" a Fake Problem?' *Columbia Journalism Review*, 31 January 2017, http://www.cjr.org/analysis/fake-news-facebook-audience-drudge-breitbart-study.php.

O'Neill, Brian, J. Ignacio Gallego and Frauke Zeller, 'New Perspectives on Audience Activity: "Prosumption" and Media Activism as Audience Practices', in Kim Christian Schrøder, Nico Carpentier and Laurie Hallett (eds), *Audience Transformations:*

Shifting Audience Positions in Late Modernity (London: Routledge, 2013).

O'Toole, Fintan, 'Denis O'Brien's Influence and the Meaning of Press Freedom', *Irish Times*, 9 June 2015, http://www.irishtimes. com/opinion/fintan-o-toole-denis-o-brien-s-influence-and-the-meaning-of-press-freedom-1.2242043.

Power, Martin J., Amanda Haynes and Eoin Devereux, 'Reasonable People vs. the Sinister Fringe: Interrogating the Framing of Ireland's Water Charge Protestors Through the Media Politics of Dissent', *Critical Discourse Studies*, vol. 13, no. 3 (2016), pp. 261–77.

Riofrancos, Thea, 'Democracy Without the People', *n+1*, 6 February 2017, https://nplusonemag.com/online-only/online-only/democracy-without-the-people/.

Rosen, Jay, 'Audience Atomization Overcome: Why the Internet Weakens the Authority of the Press', *PressThink*, 12 January 2009, http://archive.pressthink.org/2009/01/12/atomization. html.

Schudson, Michael, 'A Family of Public Spheres', Social Science Research Council, 4 August 2009, http://publicsphere.ssrc.org/ schudson-a-family-of-public-spheres/ (accessed 5 February 2017).

Siapera, Eugenia, 'Reclaiming Citizenship in the Post-Democratic Condition' *Journal of Citizenship and Globalization Studies*, vol 1, no. 1 (2017): 24–35.

Silke, Henry, 'An Attack on Democracy', *Critical Media Review*, 9 February 2015, https://criticalmediareview.wordpress. com/2015/02/09/an-attack-on-democracy/.

Simkin, John, 'William Cobbett', *Spartacus Educational*. http:// spartacus-educational.com/PRcobbett.htm (accessed 12 February 2017).

Silverman, Craig and Lawrence Alexander, 'How Teens in the Balkans Are Duping Trump Supporters With Fake News', *BuzzFeed*, 3 November 2016, https://www.buzzfeed.com/craigsilverman/how-macedonia-became-a-global-hub-for-pro-trump-misinfo.

Simplican, Stacy Clifford, *The Capacity Contract: Intellectual Disability and the Question of Citizenship* (London: University of Minnesota Press, 2015).

Streeck, Wolfgang, *How Will Capitalism End?* (London: Verso Books, 2016).

Tharoor, Ishaan, 'Viewpoint: Why Was the Biggest Protest in World History Ignored?', *Time*, 15 February 2013, http://world.time.com/2013/02/15/viewpoint-why-was-the-biggest-protest-in-world-history-ignored/.

Timberg, Craig, 'Russian Propaganda Effort Helped Spread "Fake News" during Election, Experts Say', *Washington Post*, 24 November 2016, https://www.washingtonpost.com/business/economy/russian-propaganda-effort-helped-spread-fake-news-during-election-experts-say/2016/11/24/793903b6-8a40-4ca9-b712-716af66098fe_story.html.

Titley, Gavan, 'The Debatability of Racism: Networked Participative Media and Postracialism', *Rasismista Ja Rajoista*, 17 February 2016, https://raster.fi/2016/02/17/the-debatability-of-racism-networked-participative-media-and-postracialism/.

Tyler, Patrick E., 'Threats and Responses: News Analysis; A New Power in the Streets', *New York Times*, 17 February 2003. https://www.nytimes.com/2003/02/17/world/threats-and-responses-news-analysis-a-new-power-in-the-streets.html.

Underwood, Doug, *When MBAs Rule the Newsroom: How Markets and Managers Are Shaping Today's Media* (New York: Columbia University Press, 1993).

Index